The Beginner's Guide to Todoist

Amir Salihefendic
Thomas Mailund

The Beginner's Guide to Todoist

Copyright © Thomas Mailund

Table of Contents

	Table of Contents	iii
1	The Beginner's Guide to Todoist	1
	About the authors	2
2	Getting started	3
	Setting up a Todoist account	3
	The basic interface	7
	Native apps	11
3	Basic features	21
	Tasks	21
	Projects	35
	Filters	44
4	Premium features	55
	Labels	55
	Filters	58

		Reminders	60
		Comments and file uploads	67
		Integration with mail and calendars	70
5		**Integrations**	**87**
		Mail integrations	87
		Browser extensions	88
		Speak to your personal assistant	88
		Time tracking using Toggl	89
		Automate your life using IFTTT and Zapier . .	89
6		**Working efficiently with your Inbox and your projects**	**91**
		Using your Inbox	92
		Working with your projects	95
		Breaking down tasks	97
7		**Systemist: A workflow example**	**99**
		Why would you have a workflow?	99
		Systemist	100
		Managing emails	103
		Managing chat	104
		Other workflows	104
8		**Afterword**	**107**

Chapter **1**

The Beginner's Guide to Todoist

We live in a busy age where we are constantly working on projects in parallel—whether it's at work or in our personal lives. However, it can become overwhelming or downright stressful to keep track of all we want to achieve. A surprisingly simple way to increase your productivity while reducing your stress levels is to use a simple todo list. By breaking down a complicated project into simpler tasks and then breaking these down further until each task is manageable, we take the first step in reducing the complexity of a project. It may seem simple, but by keeping a written list of your outstanding tasks, you are offloading the job of remembering these tasks from your active memory. This clarity can reduce your stress levels and make you feel more in control of your projects.

Using scraps of paper as your todo list has its drawbacks, however. It is easy to forget to bring the list with you when you're out; updating the list means rewriting it on a new piece of paper; it's easy to lose the list or destroy it in the wash. That's why digital todo-list managers are an attractive choice. Todoist is a prime contender in the market of online todo list managers, its basic features are free, you can use it across many platforms via the web or its many apps, and it integrates with more than 50 online services. This booklet is an introduction to Todoist that will guide you through setting up an account, creating, managing and completing your tasks and projects, and integrating Todoist into your daily workflow.

About the authors

Amir Salihefendic is the founder and CEO of Doist, the creators of Todoist and other productivity software that let you do more and stress less.

Thomas Mailund is an associate professor of bioinformatics at Aarhus University, Denmark, author of several textbooks, and a user of Todoist since its earliest beta versions more than ten years ago.

Chapter 2

Getting started

Todoist is an online service that works on 10+ platforms and syncs your tasks across them all. In this chapter, we get started by setting up your Todoist account and installing the Todoist apps that apply to you.

Setting up a Todoist account

To set up a Todoist account, you go to http://www.todoist.com. If this is the first time you visit the site, the front page will look like the picture below. To set up an account, you should click the "Get Started - It's Free" button.

Clicking the button will take you to a sign-up form. Here, you can use an existing Google or Facebook account to create your Todoist account, or you can type in an email address and a password.

If you sign up using a Google or Facebook account, you need

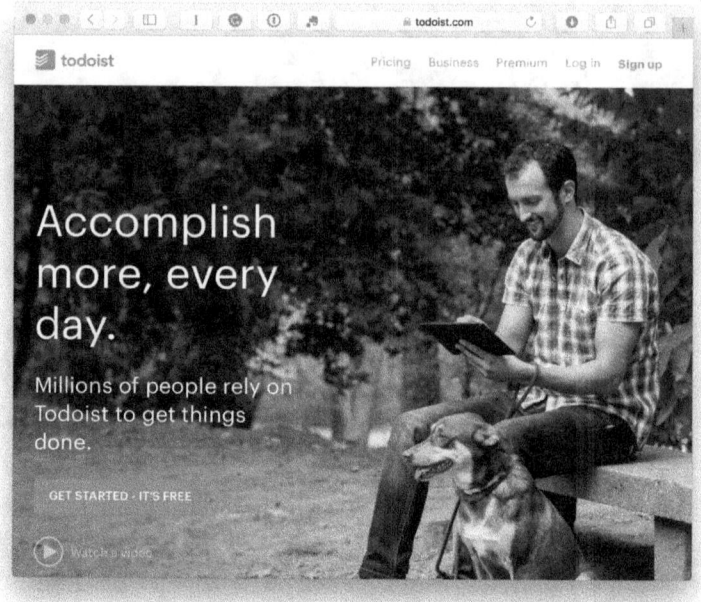

Figure 1: Todoist webpage.

to give Todoist permission to access your credentials from those services, and after that, you can log into Todoist using them. If you sign up using an email address, you just need to remember the password you provide to be able to log in later.

Regardless of how you chose to sign up, you will be sent to a signup wizard. Click the "Let's Go" button to get started.

The first choice you get to make during sign up is the theme Todoist will use when it shows you your todo-lists. You can choose whatever color you'd like, and don't worry if you

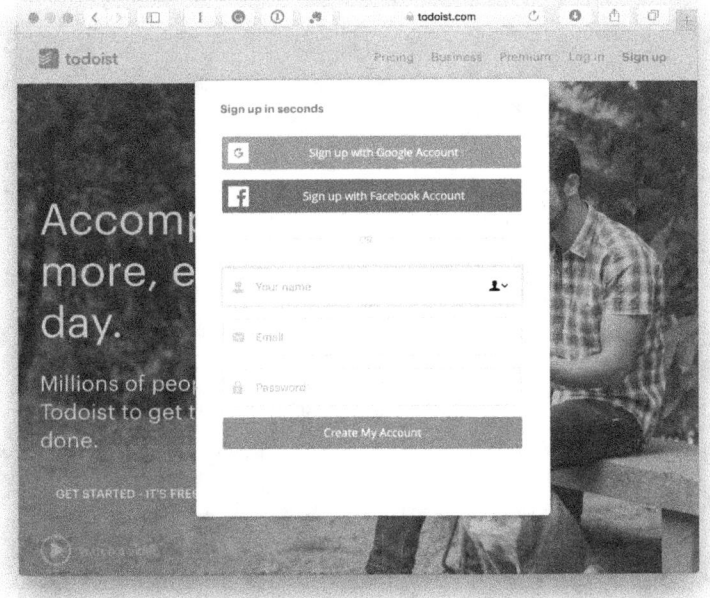

Figure 2: Todoist sign-up.

change your mind, you can always choose a new color later.

After that, you will be asked to add a task for today. Just type anything here—it is just used as an example, so it isn't so important what you choose.

Your third choice is to add a daily task. Daily are tasks that will be added to your todo-list each day—if you complete them, they will be added again the next day, if you do not complete them, they are moved to your overdue tasks but not added again for each day.

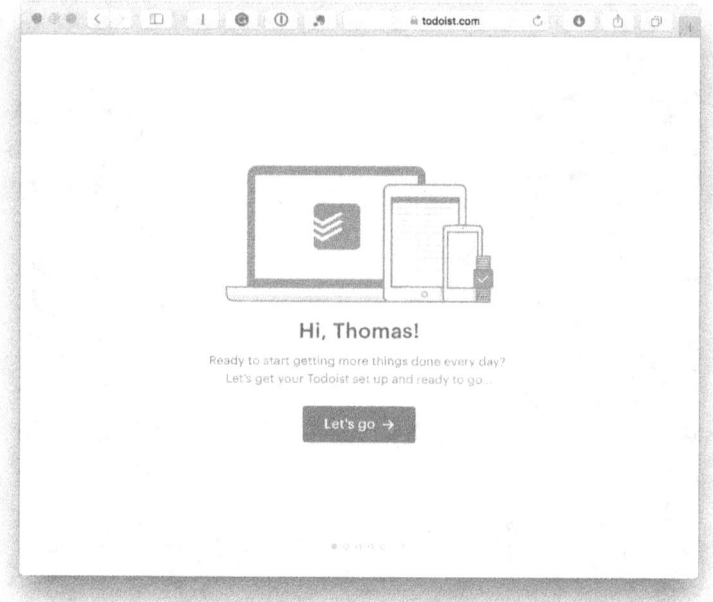

Figure 3: Signup wizard.

Since the task is just there as an example of repeated tasks, you can write anything and delete it later.

After adding the two tasks, you are done with the sign-up. You can choose to subscribe to the Todoist blog if you're interested in productivity tricks and news about Todoist or you can choose not to subscribe.

Clicking the "Finish" button will send you to the main Todoist interface where you can see all your projects and tasks.

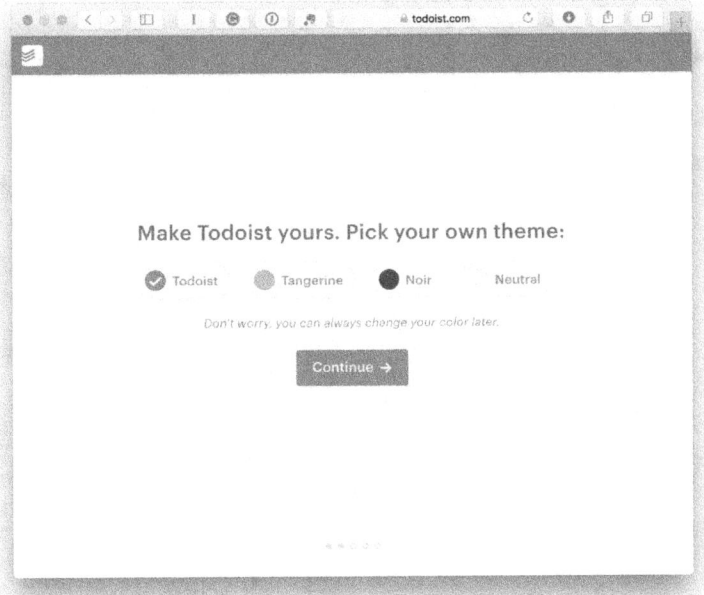

Figure 4: Pick your theme.

The basic interface

This interface shows you a list of projects on the left—there are some default projects already defined when you sign up, but you can always change them.

If you click on any of the projects, you will be shown the tasks associated with the selected project. Right now, though, none of the projects has any tasks associated—you are being shown the two tasks you created when signing up as part of today's

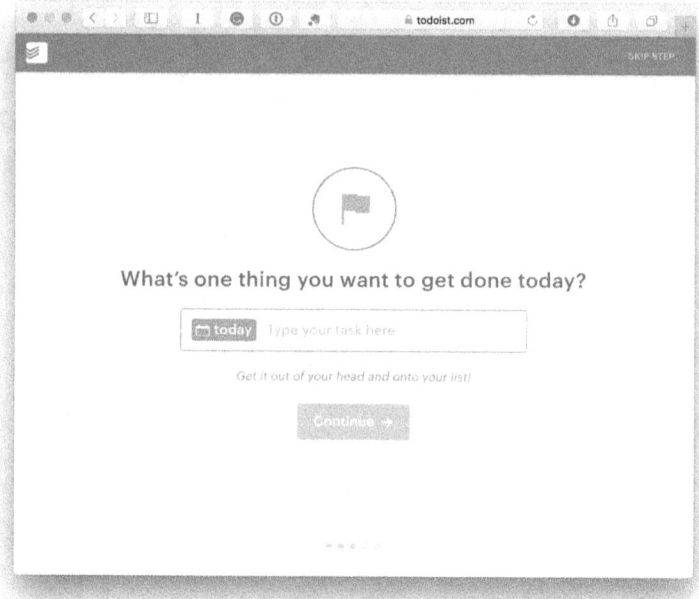

Figure 5: Add a task for today.

tasks and these are part of the special project "Inbox".

There are three useful task views that are not directly associated with projects: Your Inbox, your tasks for today, and your tasks for the next seven days. You can pick between these three views at the upper left of the window.

The Inbox is where tasks are put by default. It behaves like a project, but it isn't intended as one. Think of it as a place where you put tasks during the day to sort them into appropriate projects at a later point. This separates the job

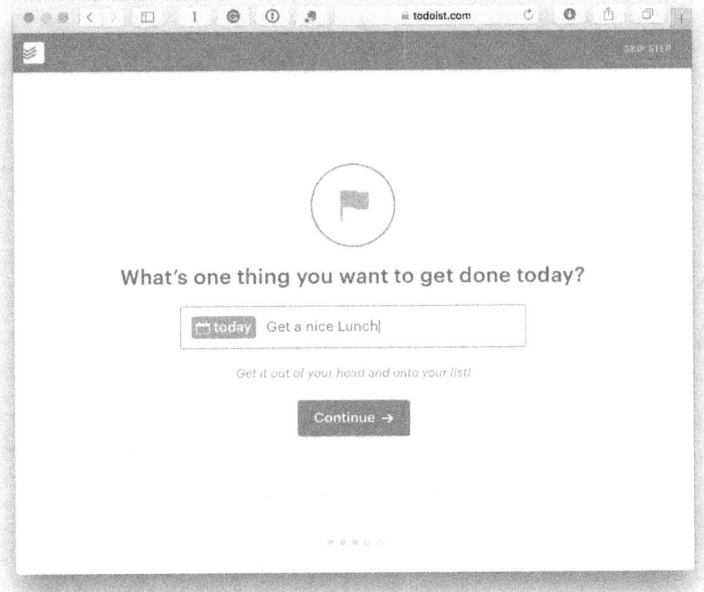

Figure 6: The task we chose for today.

of adding tasks from organising your todo-list. The "Today" and "Next 7 days" folders should be self-explanatory.

When you have just logged in for the first time, you are shown the tasks for today. The tasks are listed at the right of the window.

If you move your cursor to the right of a task, three dots will appear.

If you click on the three dots, a drop-down menu appears.

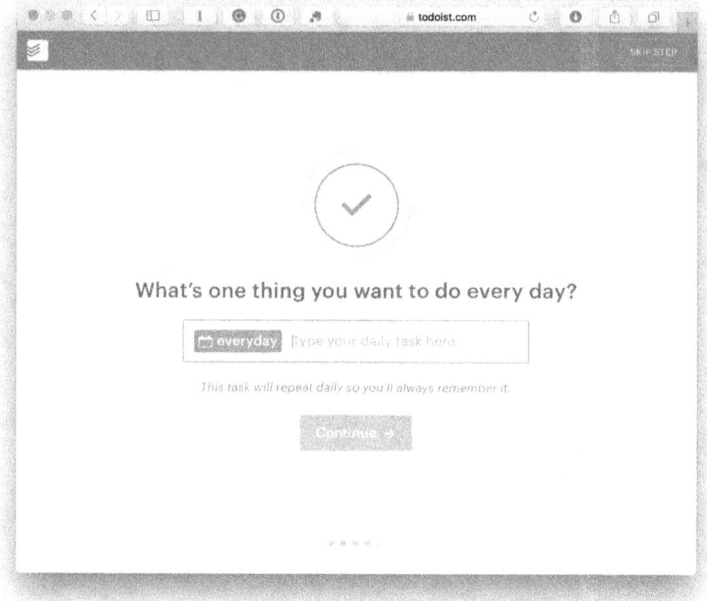

Figure 7: Add a repeating task.

You can use this menu to edit tasks.

You can, for example, use the menu to assign a task to a project. Just click "Move to another project", and a list of your projects appear.

You can also choose to delete a task from this drop-down menu.

If you want to get rid of the daily task that you added when you signed up, this is the place to do it. If you just complete it,

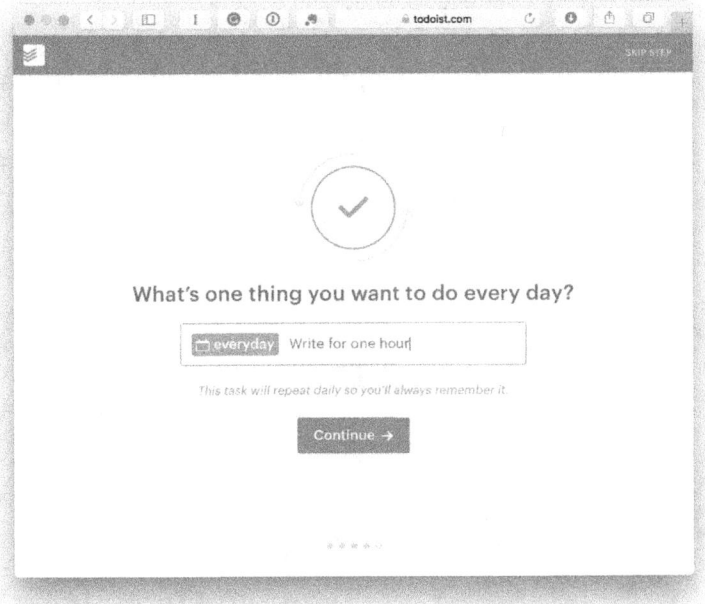

Figure 8: The task you chose to repeat every day.

which you can do by clicking the circle to the left of the task, it will disappear from today's tasks but reappear tomorrow. If you delete it, you get rid of it.

Native apps

In many cases, working with Todoist through your web browser is a convenient choice, but if you are on the road and not always online, you might want to install it as a native app, where

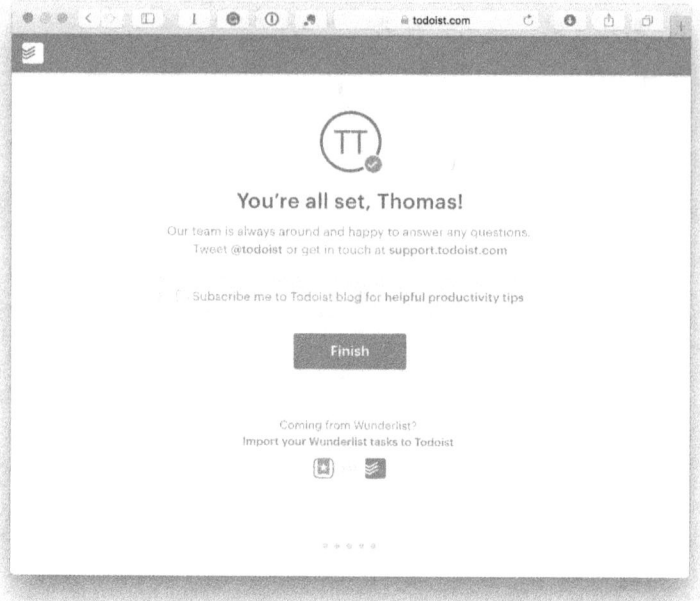

Figure 9: Welcome screen.

you can work with Todoist offline. You can get apps for different platforms by going to https://en.todoist.com/downloads. There are desktop apps for MacOS and Windows, mobile apps for iOS and Android, and even wearable apps for iWatch and Android Wear. On the same page, you can get browser extensions for integrating Chrome, Safari, or Firefox with Todoist—making it easy to turn web pages into tasks. You can also get plugins for integrating Outlook or Gmail with Todoist, making it easy to translate emails into tasks.

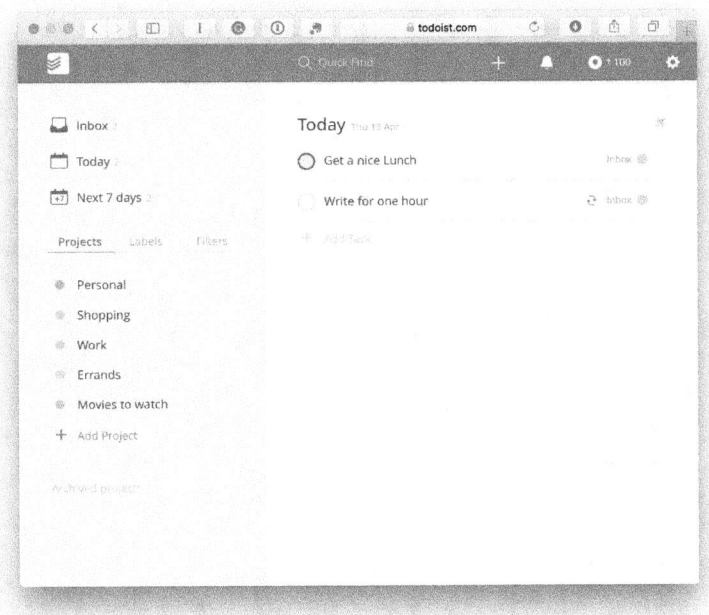

Figure 10: Main Todoist lists.

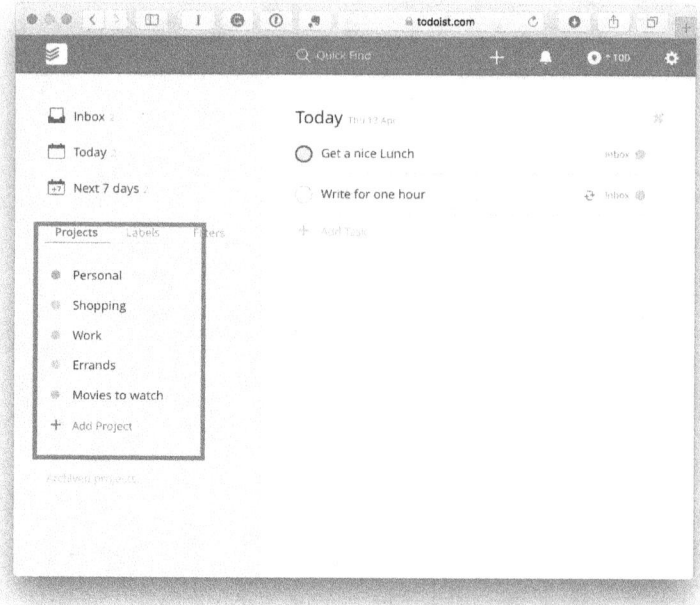

Figure 11: Your Todoist projects.

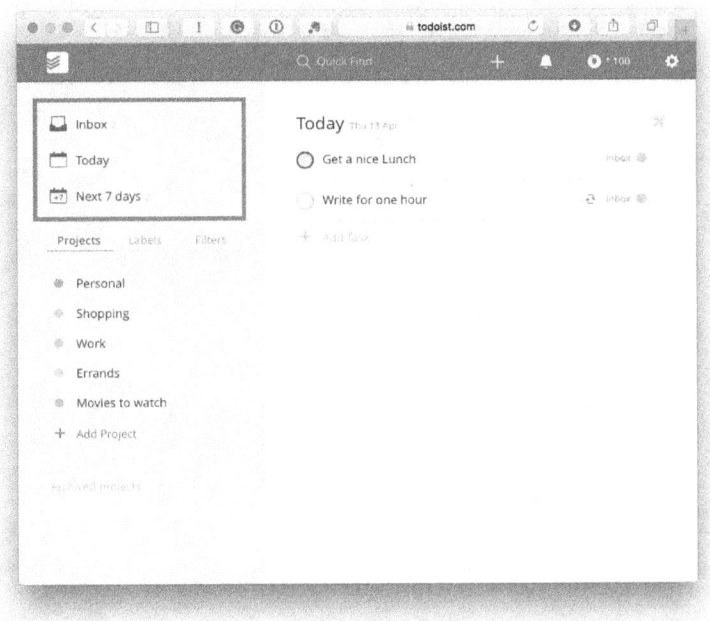

Figure 12: Special lists: Inbox, Today and Next 7 days

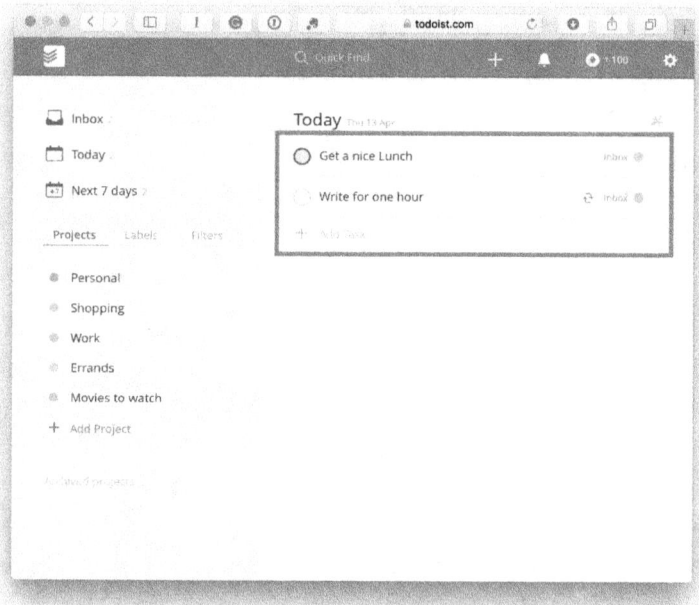

Figure 13: Your tasks for today.

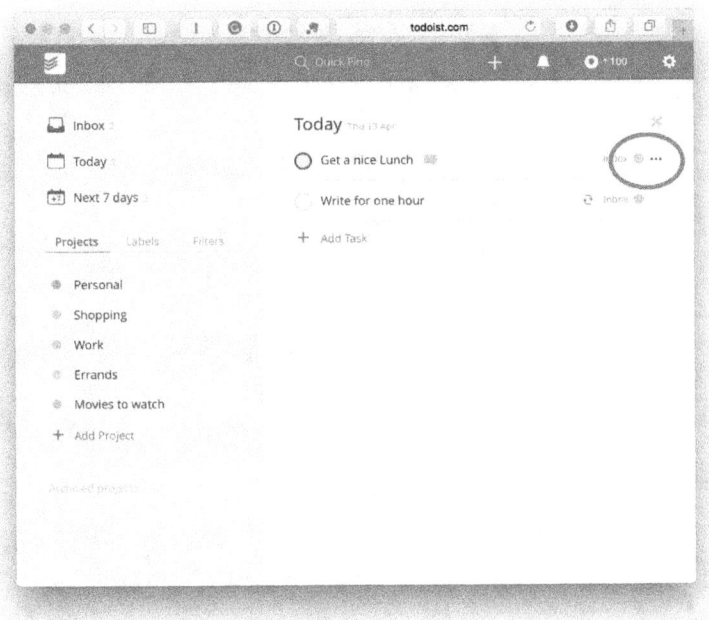

Figure 14: Open task options.

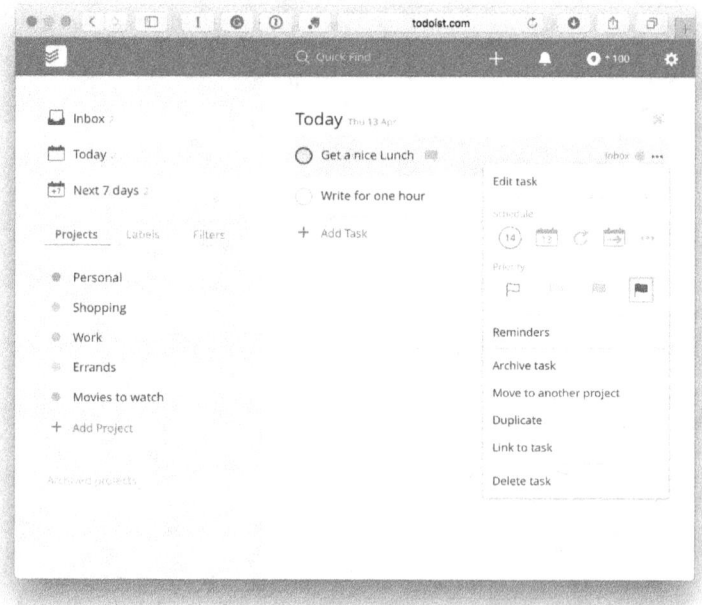

Figure 15: Task options.

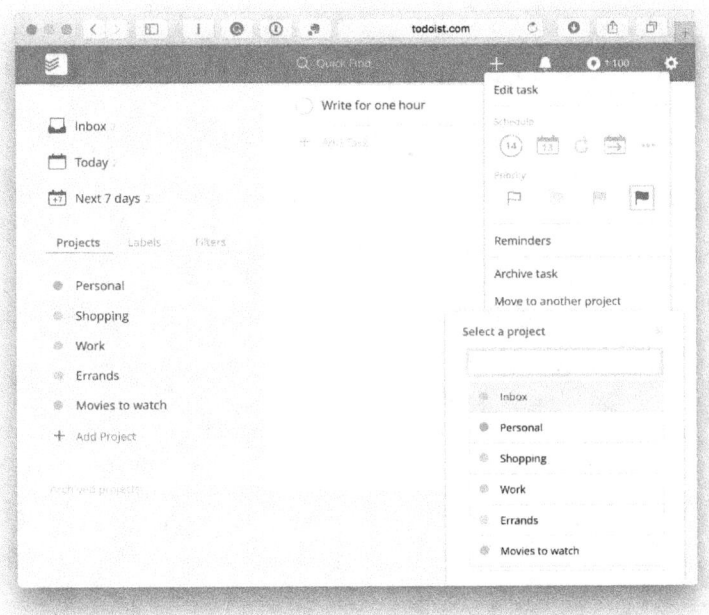

Figure 16: Moving a task to a different project.

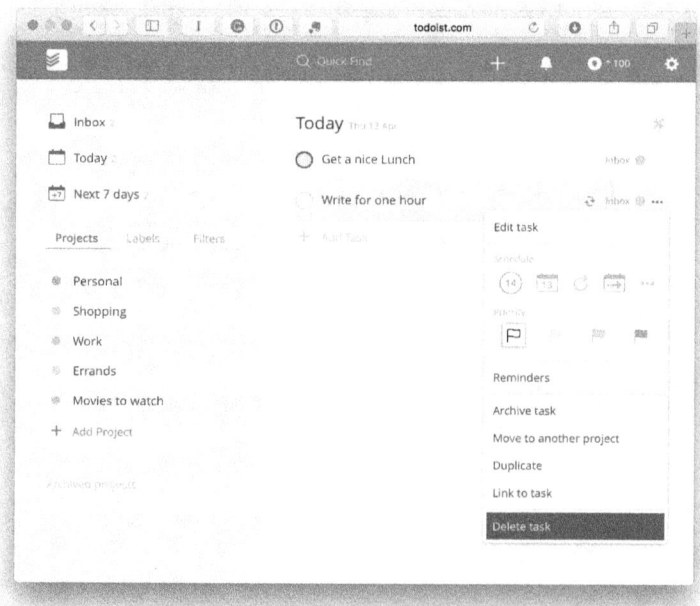

Figure 17: Deleting a task.

Chapter **3**

Basic features

In this chapter, we will go through the basic features available in a free Todoist account. For most users, these will suffice to increase your productivity, but for those of you who are looking for more, we examine the features available in a premium subscription in the next chapter.

Tasks

If you have completed the default tasks you created when you signed up for your Todoist account (you do this by clicking on the circle to the left of the task title) or if you have simply deleted all of your tasks, you should have an empty list of today's tasks.

This empty list is where you want to be at the end of each day, after you've completed all of your tasks. However, you will only be productive if you actually add some tasks first so

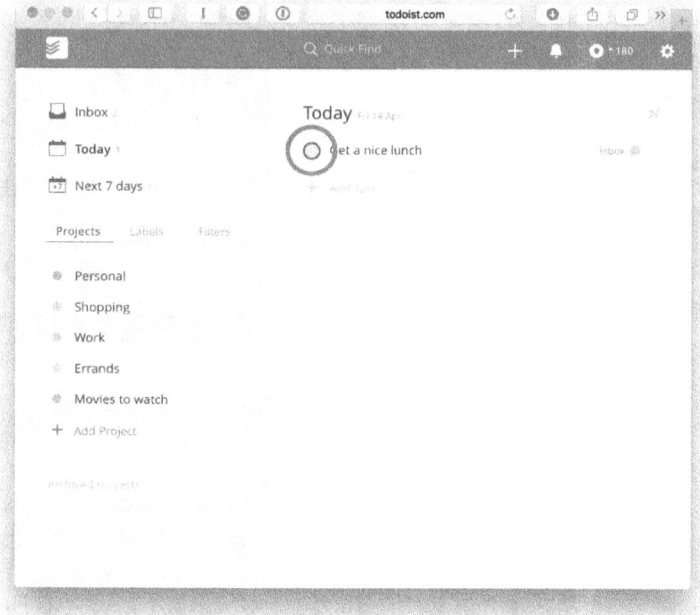

Figure 18: Completing a task.

you have something to mark as completed. A task list is only as effective as the tasks you choose to add.

To add a new task, you can click on the "Add task" link.

This presents you with a field where you can write out the title of the task and select the date it should be completed. If you are in the Today view when you add the task, the completion date defaults to the current date; otherwise, the completion date will be empty.

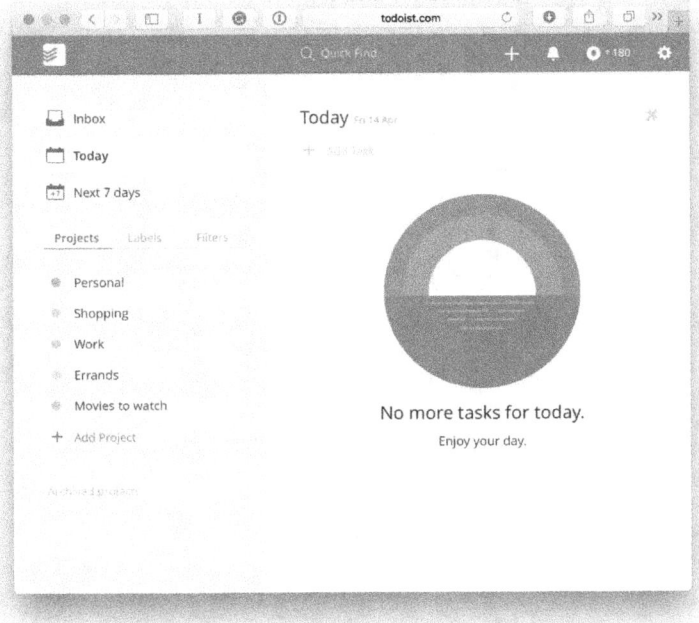

Figure 19: An empty Today's tasks list.

You can also "quick add" a task using the keyboard shortcut Q. Here, you have the same options as if you add a task in the Today's list, but the task will, by default, be added to the Inbox list, even if you are currently looking at Today's list or a project, and the completion date will not be automatically set.

Anyway, let us just add a task in the Today's list for now. Just type in a title for the task. Then hit Enter.

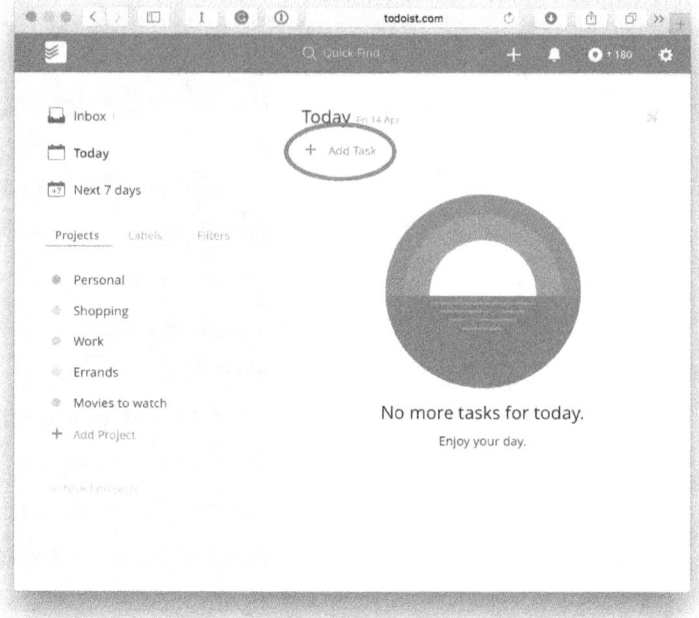

Figure 20: Add task button.

After hitting Enter, you will have a new task open so you can continue adding more and more tasks.

You can just cancel the new task, either by clicking on Cancel or by hitting the Esc key. If you just added a single task, and you added it in the Today list, you should have a list that looks like this:

When you write out the title of a task, Todoist will try to understand some of what you write and use it as meta-

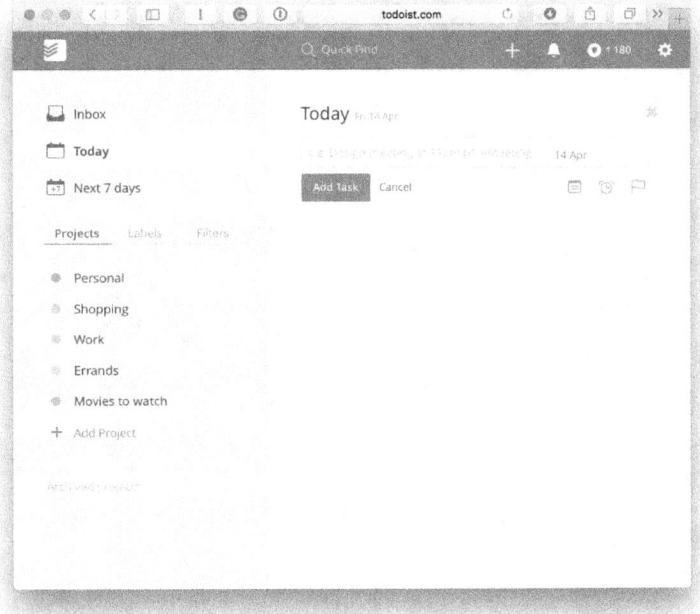

Figure 21: Add task.

information. If you write something that can be interpreted as a date—like "today", "tomorrow", "next Sunday", "April 15"—it will interpret this and set your completion date as such. You can also add recurring due dates to your tasks like "every first of the month" or "every Monday".

You can add a time for a task as well as a date. To do this, just write a complete date as normal but follow it with "@" and then a time point. You can set the time from within the

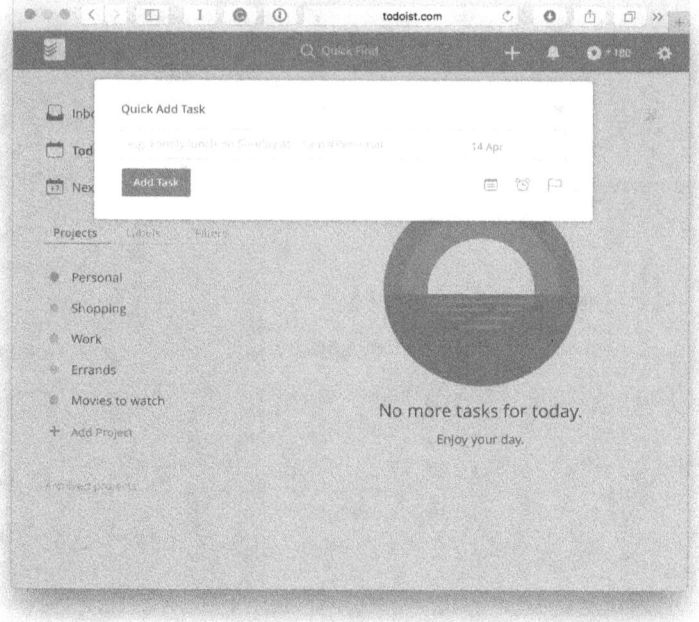

Figure 22: Quick add task.

input text box or you can set it from the date scheduler.

If you have successfully added a time as well as a date, you will see this when the task has been added.

If you want to put the task in a project—more on projects below—you can write a hash-tag and then the project name, e.g. `#Personal`.

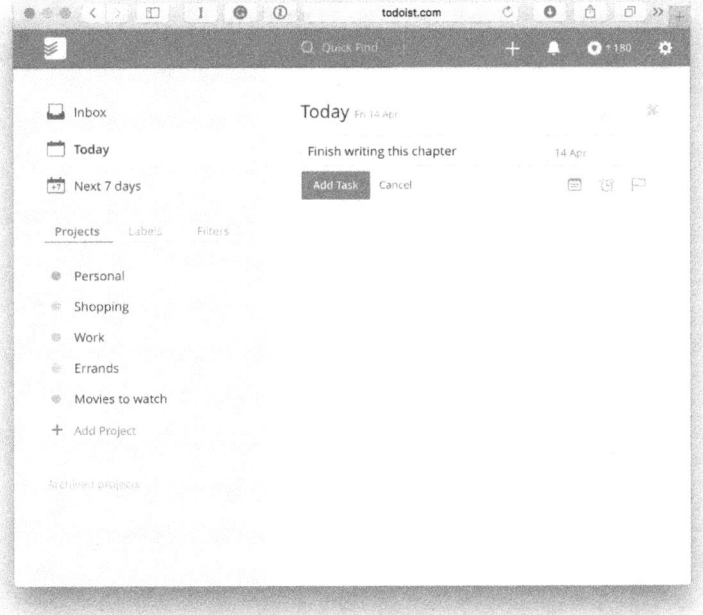

Figure 23: Adding a task.

Setting task priorities

When you create a task, you can give it a priority by clicking on the flag to the bottom right of where you write the task title.

This opens a small dialogue where you can select four different levels of priority.

Since you are already typing in the task title, though, it's

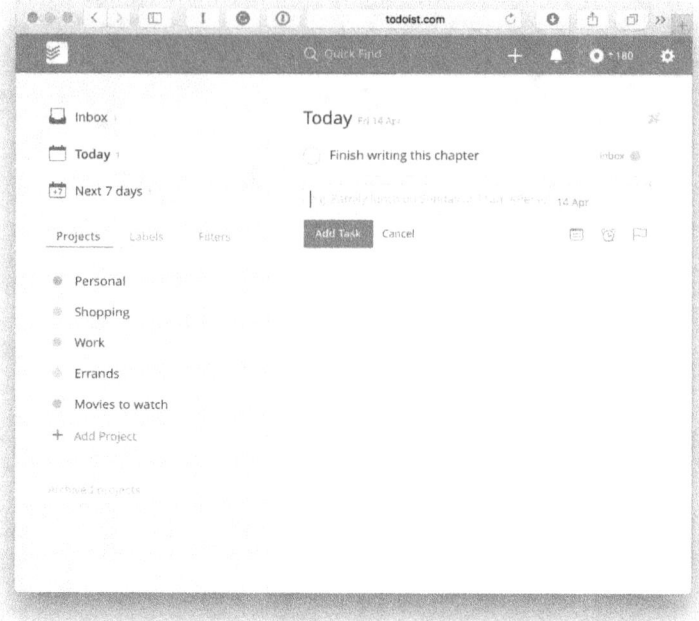

Figure 24: Adding additional tasks.

much easier to add a priority by typing "p1", "p2", "p3", or "p4" to pick the priority level.

Rescheduling tasks

You don't necessarily want to schedule an end date for all tasks. Quite often, a project has many tasks and you don't necessarily want to schedule every single one right away. Some of the tasks have dependencies or are too distant to start

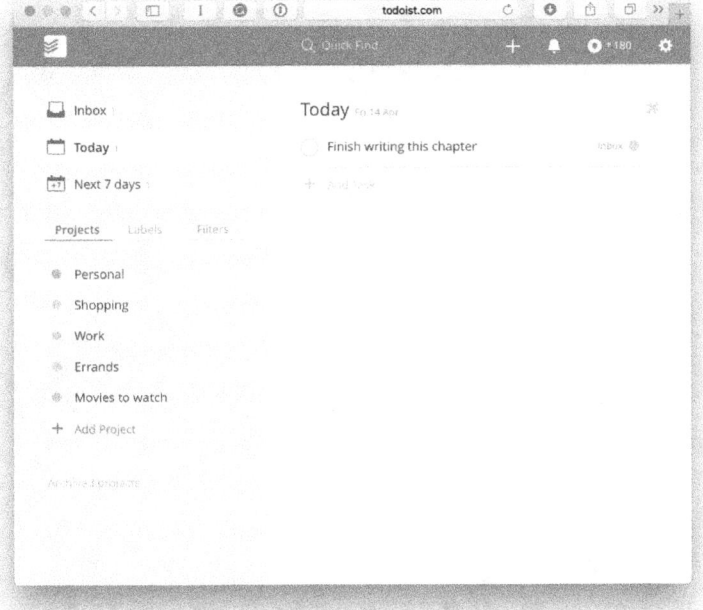

Figure 25: Done adding tasks.

scheduling.

However, there will inevitably be times where you set a completion date for a task and when the date arrives, you haven't managed to complete it. That leaves you with an overdue task.

If you click on the three dots to the right of the task title you open the menu for editing the task. In this menu there are a series of quick action buttons that allow you to reschedule

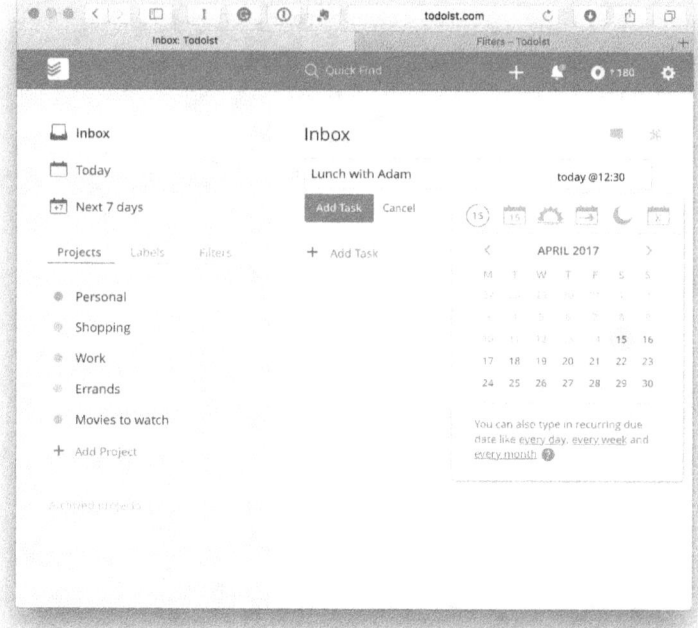

Figure 26: Adding time time a task.

the task to tomorrow, next week or next month. If you want a specific date, you can select the option "More", whose icon is again the three dots.

Clicking there opens a calendar where you can reschedule the task.

Rescheduling a single task is relatively simple, but if you're behind on a few projects you may have many overdue tasks,

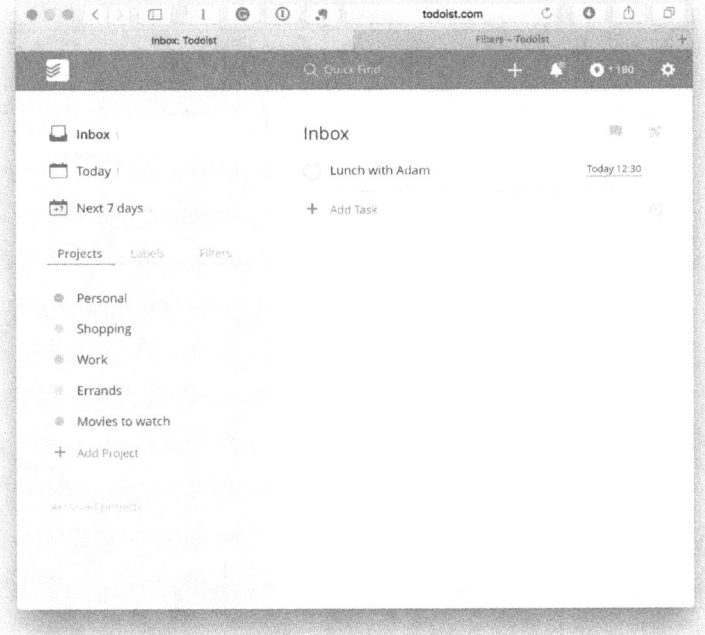

Figure 27: A task with an associated time.

which isn't as easy to reschedule. For this case, Todoist offers an AI-based rescheduling option. To the top-right of the list of overdue tasks, you can click on Reschedule overdue.

The first time you do this, you get a dialogue where you can get more information and where you can sign up to the service.

If you accept to use the AI, and any time after you have

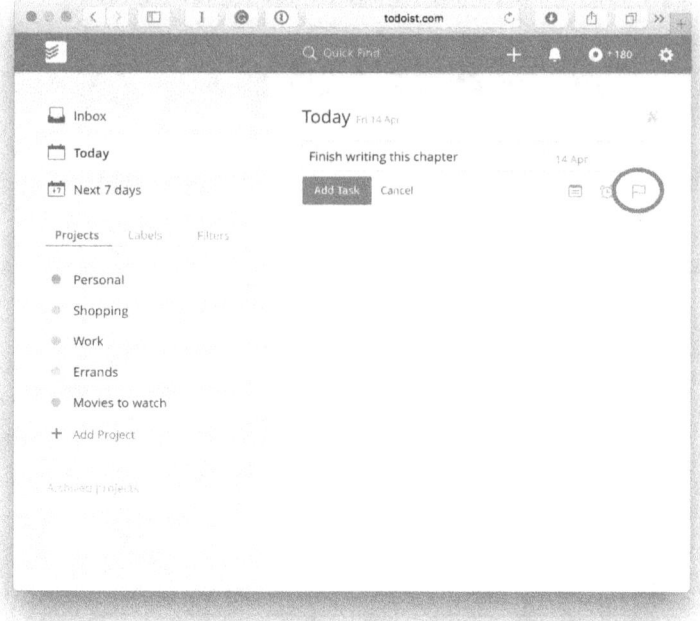

Figure 28: Open priority options.

accepted it and click Reschedule overdue, you will be presented with a list of suggested dates for your overdue tasks.

The reschedule suggestions will be based on your typical rescheduling patterns for project and kinds of tasks and will improve as the AI learns more about your work patterns.

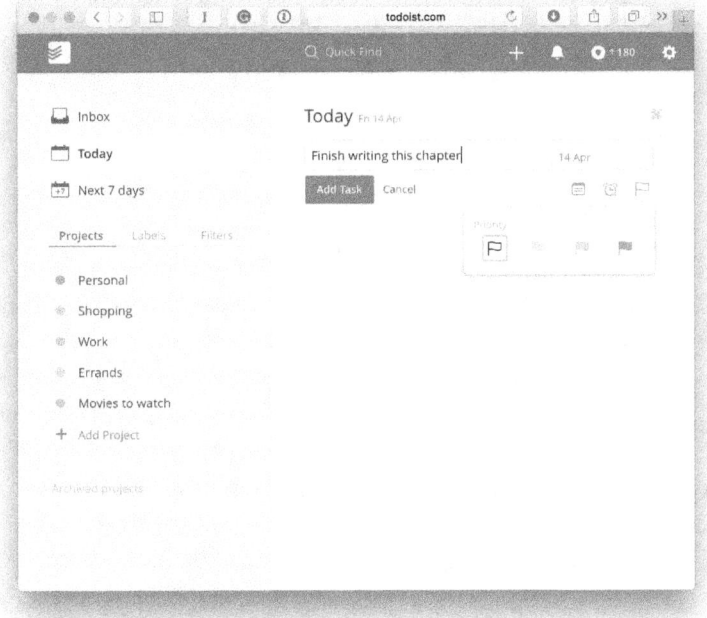

Figure 29: Selecting a priority.

Creating tasks with sub-tasks

If you move your pointer to the left of a task title, you will see a handle for moving the task around, which works differently in different contexts.

In the Today task view, you can drag a task to the bottom of the list to postpone it to tomorrow. In the Next 7 days task view, you can drag tasks to different completion dates.

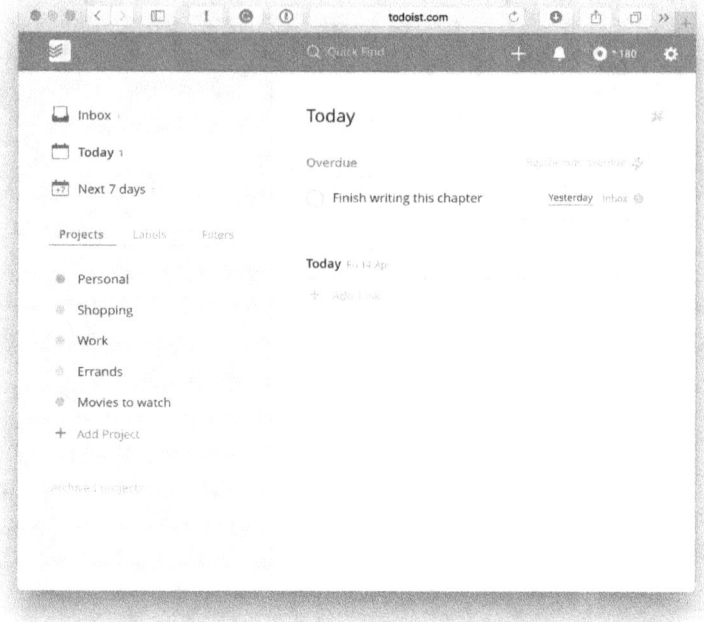

Figure 30: An overdue task.

If you are in the Inbox view, or any of your specific projects, you can drag tasks between projects but you can also turn tasks into the subtasks of other tasks.

To make a task into a subtask, you can drag it in under the parent task and drag it slightly to the right to indent it. You can nest tasks and subtasks as deep as you want. Keep in mind that this only works in the Inbox or within a project view.

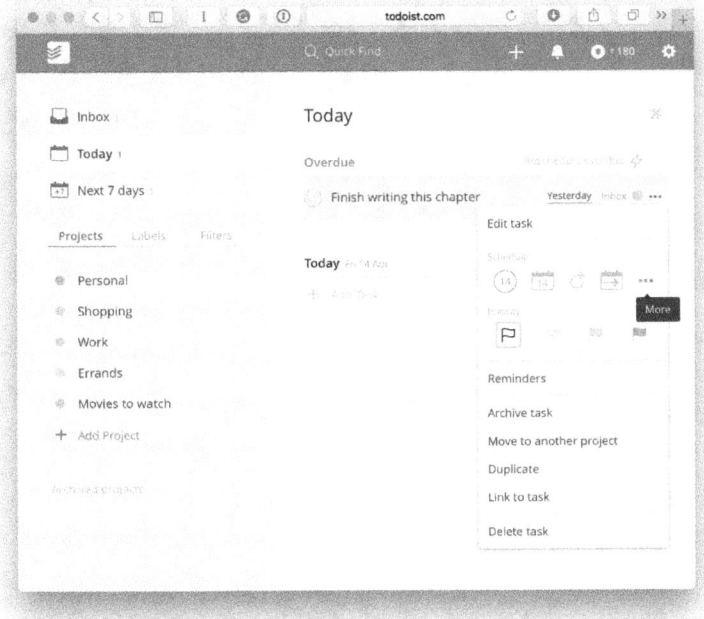

Figure 31: Moving a task to a later date.

Projects

Your list of projects is shown on the bottom left pane of the Todoist window.

These can be used to organise your tasks in a similar way to how you organise files in directories or photos in albums. You can have as many projects as you want and you can organise them into subprojects if you'd like. However, you probably shouldn't overthink the project organisation. If you

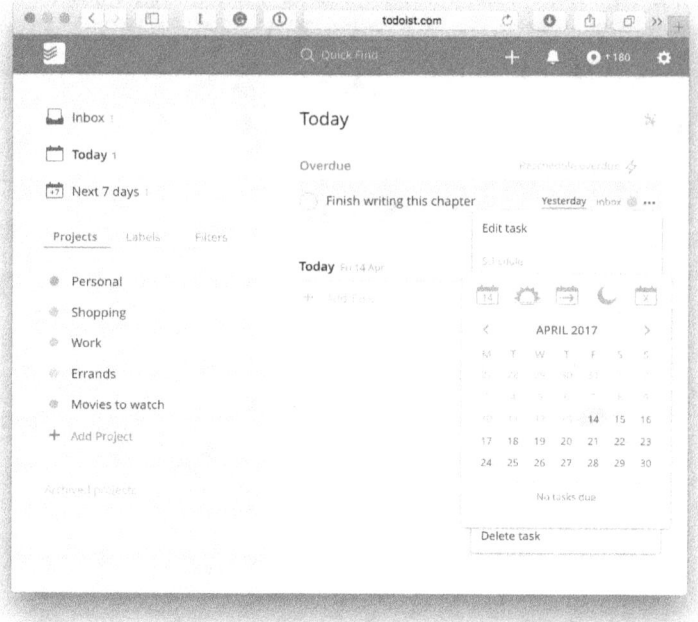

Figure 32: The task calendar.

have too many projects with too complex a structure, your todo lists become overly complex and difficult to navigate, and rather than assisting you in increasing your productivity, they begin to slow you down as you search for the project you need. It makes sense to use projects for long-term work; you're probably better to use tasks and subtasks for work you will complete in a few weeks or a few months. Of course, experiment to find out what works best for you.

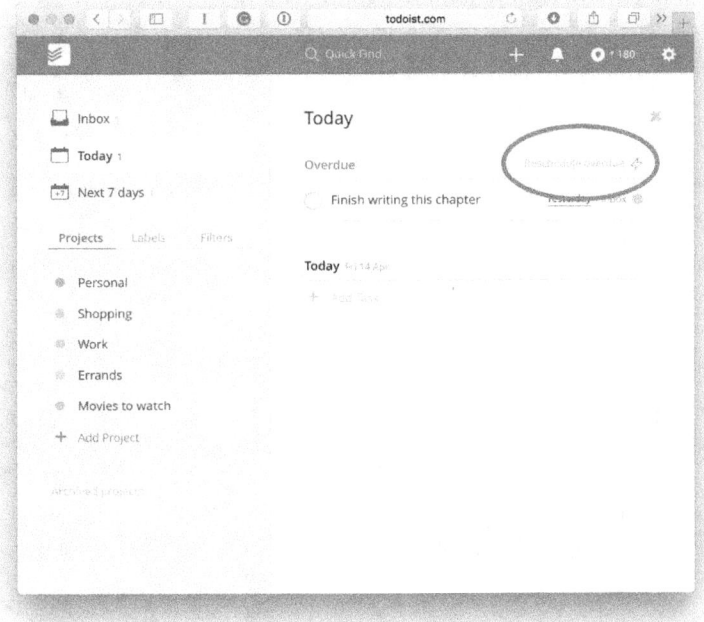

Figure 33: Automatic rescheduling.

Your new Todoist account comes with a few sample projects already defined. You can add more by clicking on Add Project and you can edit or delete the existing projects by clicking on the three dots that appear when you move your pointer over a project title. We go into more detail below.

From the menu, the two topmost menu items allow you to add a project adjacent to the currently selected project. However, it's easy to move projects around and make projects into

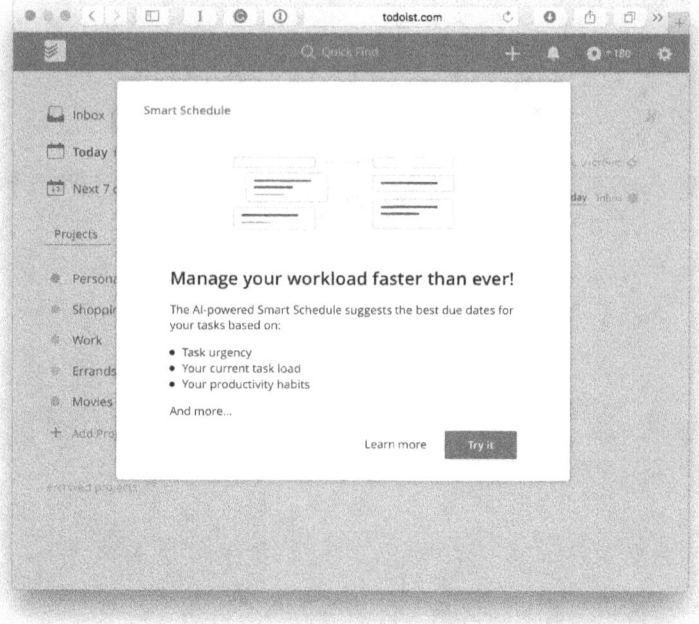

Figure 34: Automatic scheduling information.

sub-projects using the handle that appears when you move the pointer over a project title. You can also use Add Project to create a project, then move it around as you like.

The next menu item, Edit project allows you to change the level at which a project is nested with the indent and unindent buttons. You can also rename the project, or change the colour of the project by clicking the dot to the left of the project name.

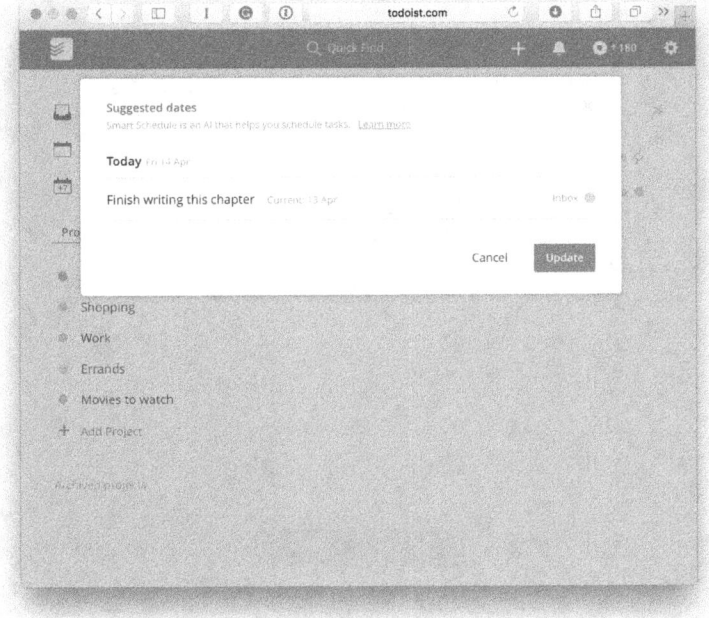

Figure 35: Rescheduling suggestions.

There is also an item for sharing a project. If you select a project—by clicking on its title—you can also share it using the "person-plus" button at the top right of the task view window.

We will return to sharing projects shortly.

The next two menu items, emailing tasks to a project and setting up a calendar feed, are premium features and covered in the next chapter. The last two menu items are two ways

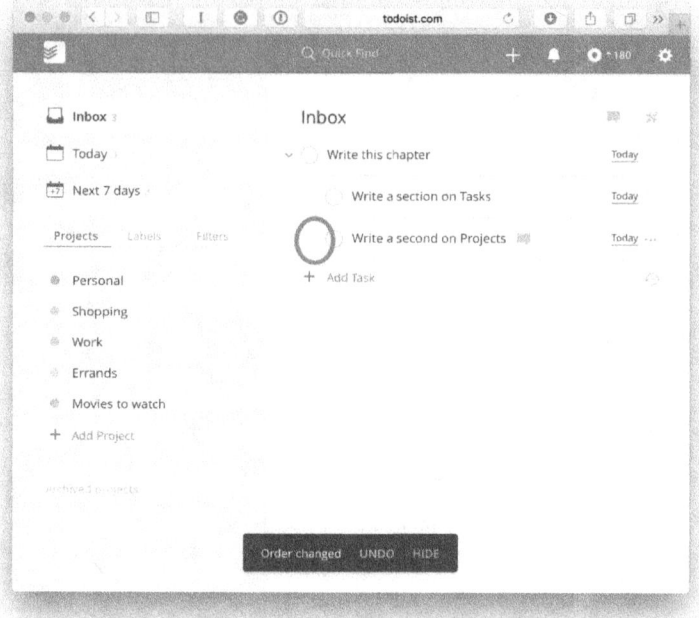

Figure 36: The movement handle.

of getting rid of a project. You can archive it, and if you do you can get it back again by clicking on the Archived projects link below the projects list. If you delete a project, it, and all its tasks, are permanently gone.

Sharing a project

Sharing projects is a feature for collaboration. If you select a project, you can share it with someone else by clicking the

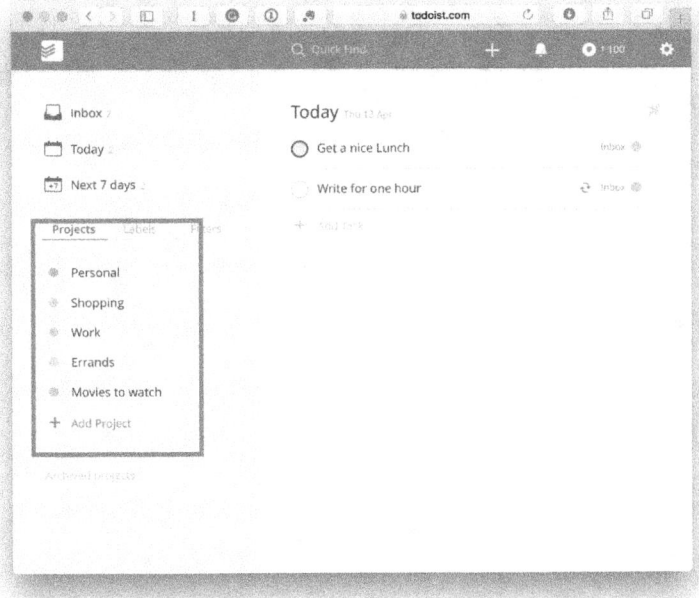

Figure 37: Projects list.

share button.

To share with someone you need to know the email address they have used to set up their Todoist account or have shared a project with them earlier, in which case you can search for them by name. [1]

If you click Invite From Project you can also get a list of

---

[1] If you have signed up using your Facebook or Google account, you need to have an email account associated with that account for sharing to work.

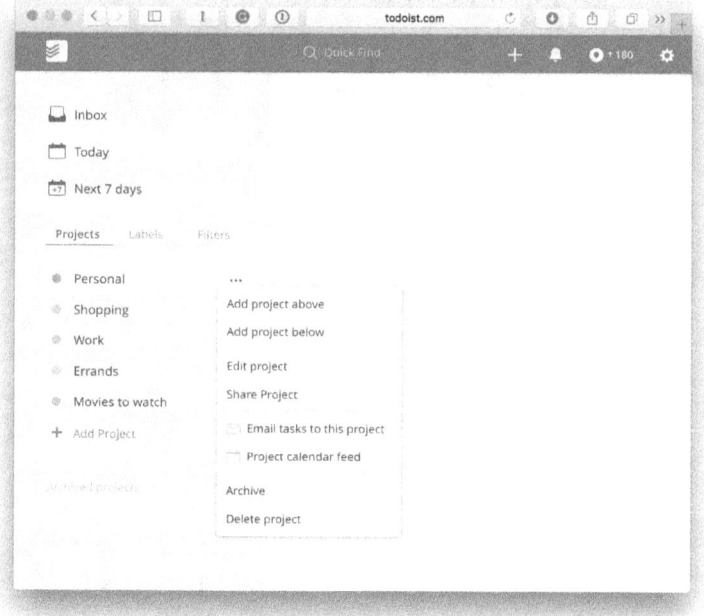

Figure 38: Editing a project.

people you have shared other projects with—if you have any such projects—and then invite all or a selected subset of participants from other projects.

After you invite someone, you will see them listed as collaborators, but pending until they accept the invitation.

You will get a notification when an invitation is accepted.

A shared project is shown with a slightly different icon—a person instead of a circle—and with shared projects, you have

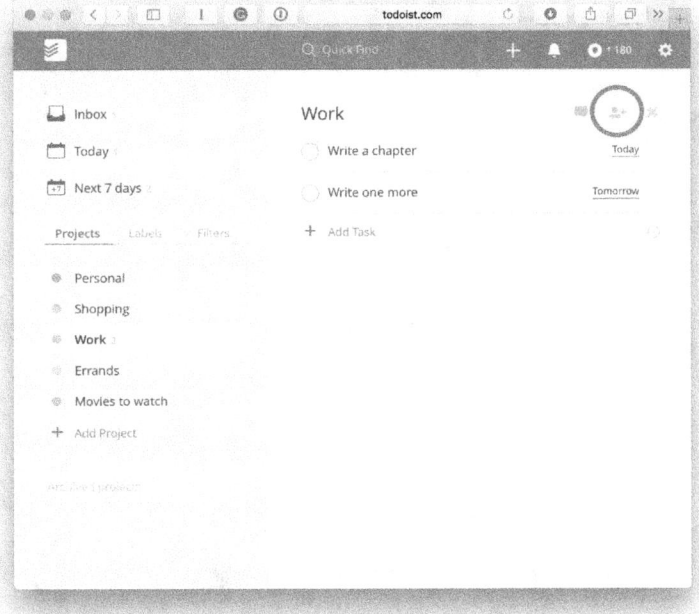

Figure 39: Sharing a project.

the option of assigning people to different tasks.

If you click on the assign icon, you can choose yourself or one of your collaborators as responsible for the task.

If you click on the project comments icon on the top of a shared project window you can start a project conversation.

An actual project conversation is straightforward.

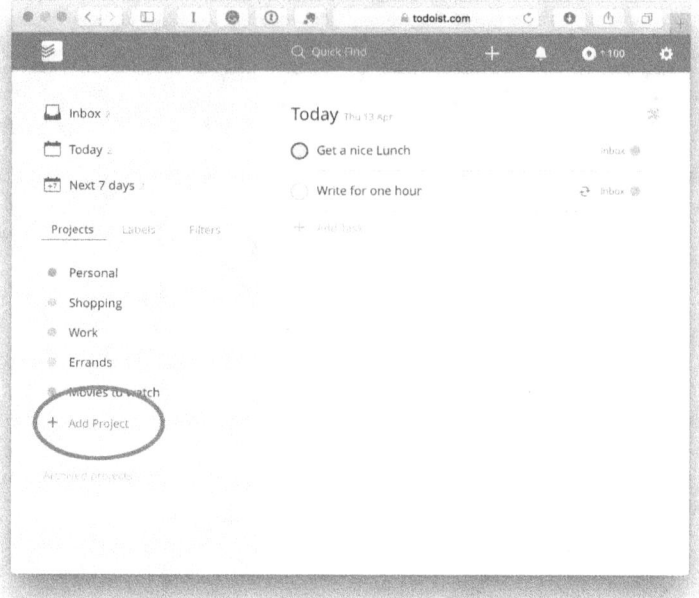

Figure 40: Archived projects.

Filters

The final basic feature is filters. If you click on the Filters label on the right of the Todoist window you will get a list of your filters.

It is possible to construct custom filters, but this is a premium feature, so we return to that in the next chapter. The basic filters you have available allows you to get a list of tasks assigned to yourself, assigned to anyone else, a list of tasks

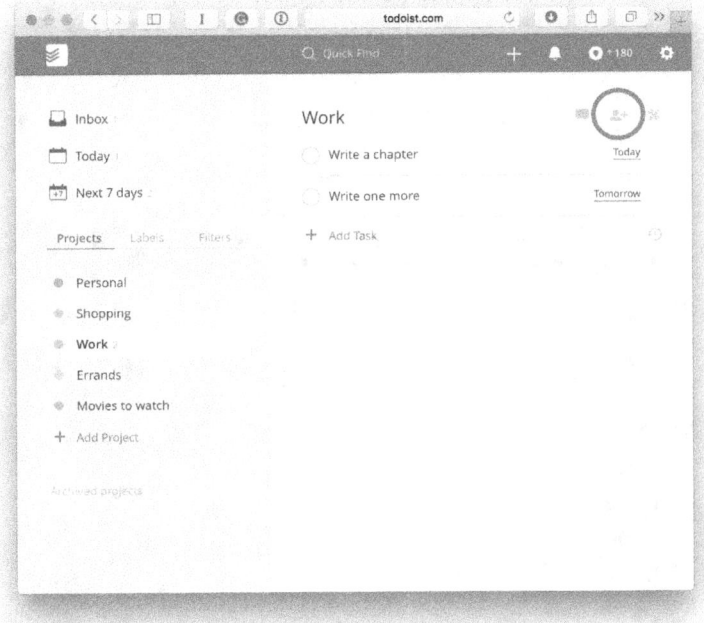

Figure 41: Sharing a project.

at each priority, all tasks whatsoever, and all tasks without a due date.

With just the basic account, filters are not as useful as they could be. Filters let you construct queries that work as smart projects, but to get use out of this you want to be able to add labels to tasks and construct filters based on them, and both these features are available only with a premium account.

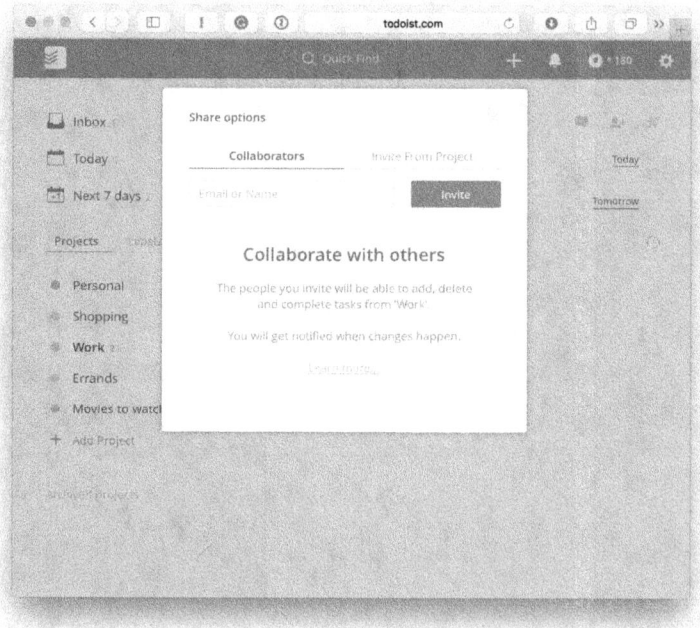

Figure 42: Send collaboration invitation.

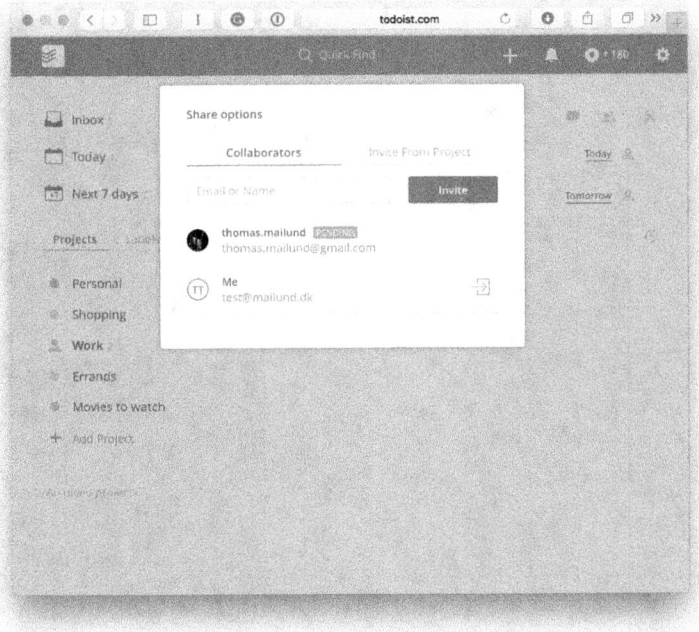

Figure 43: Collaborator's acceptance is pending.

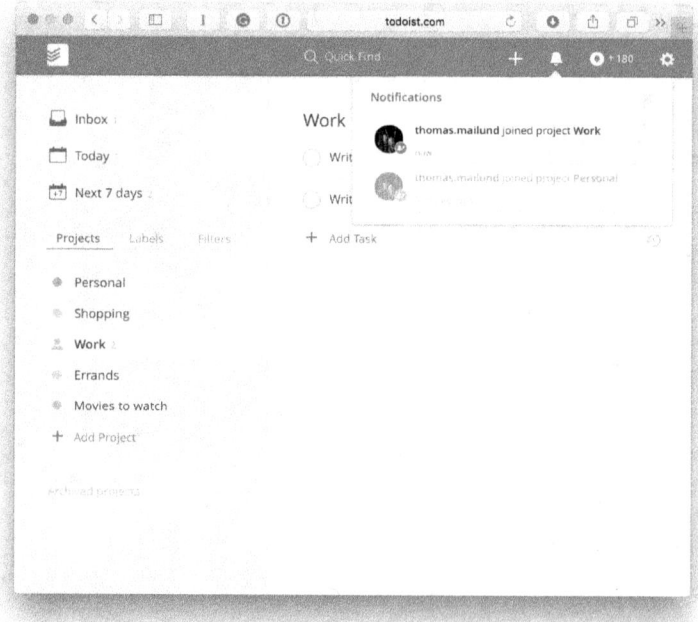

Figure 44: Collaboration has accepted the invitation.

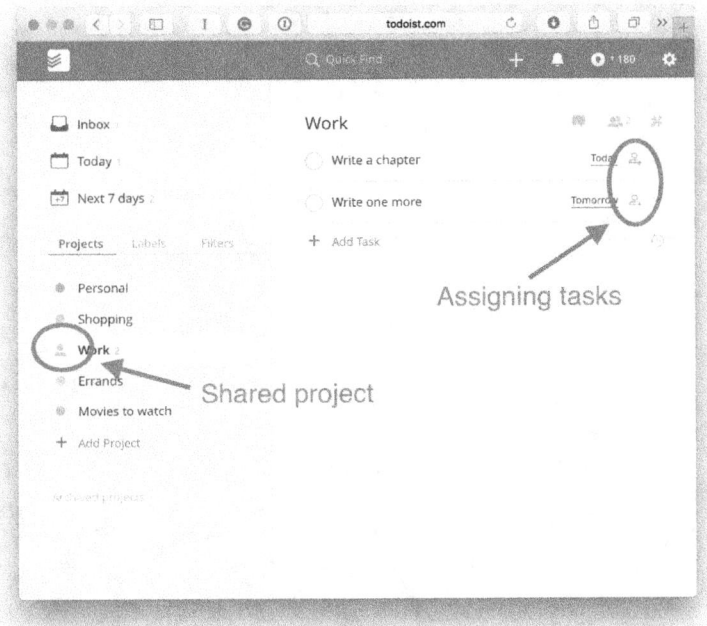

Figure 45: Shared project.

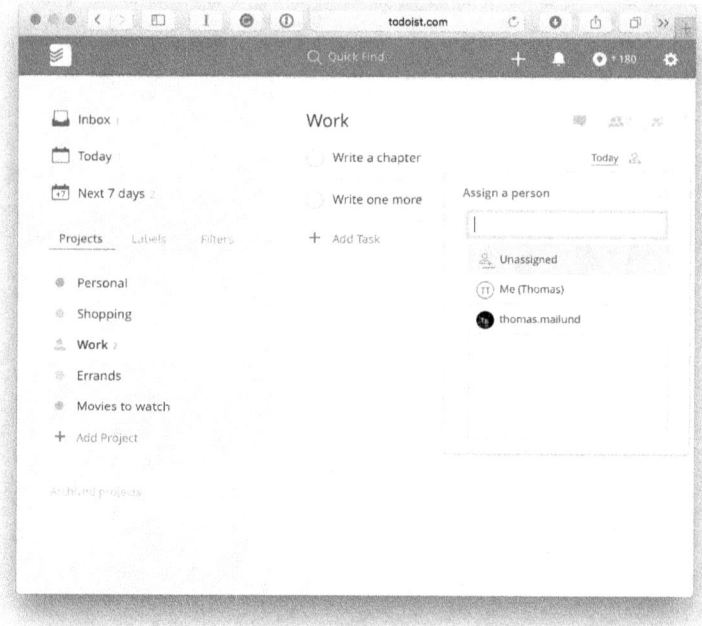

Figure 46: Assigning a task.

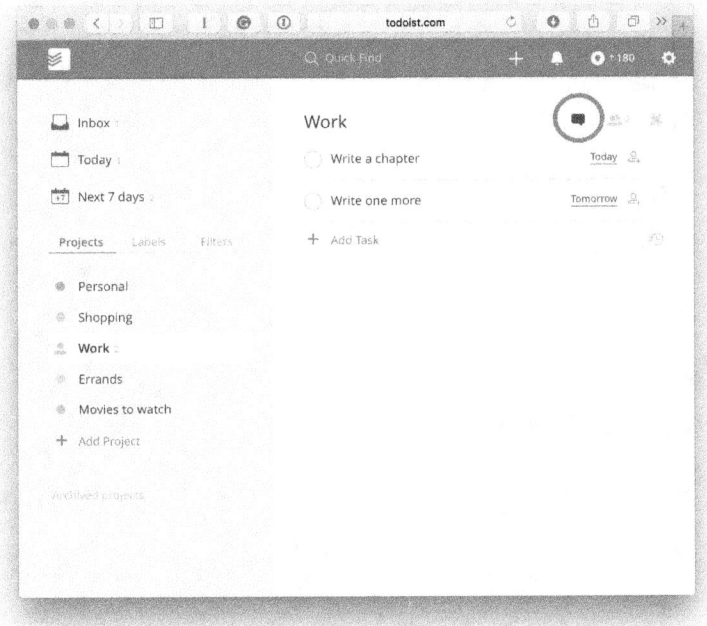

Figure 47: Project comments.

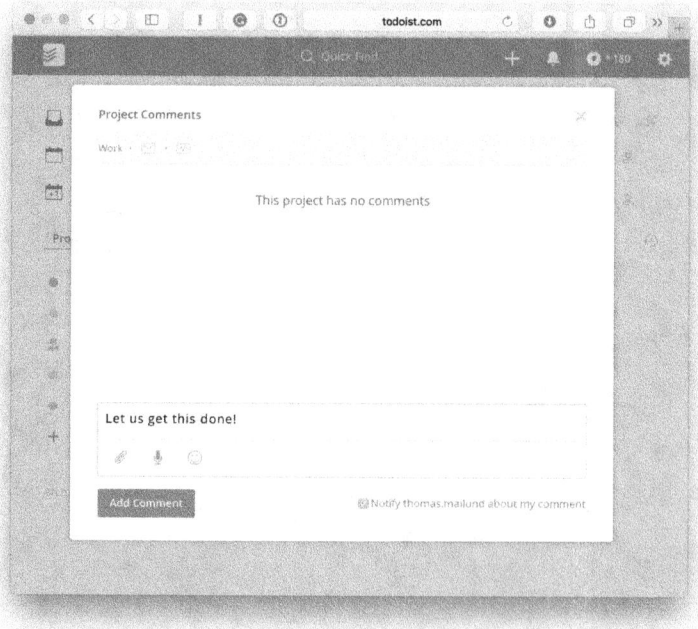

Figure 48: Writing a project comment.

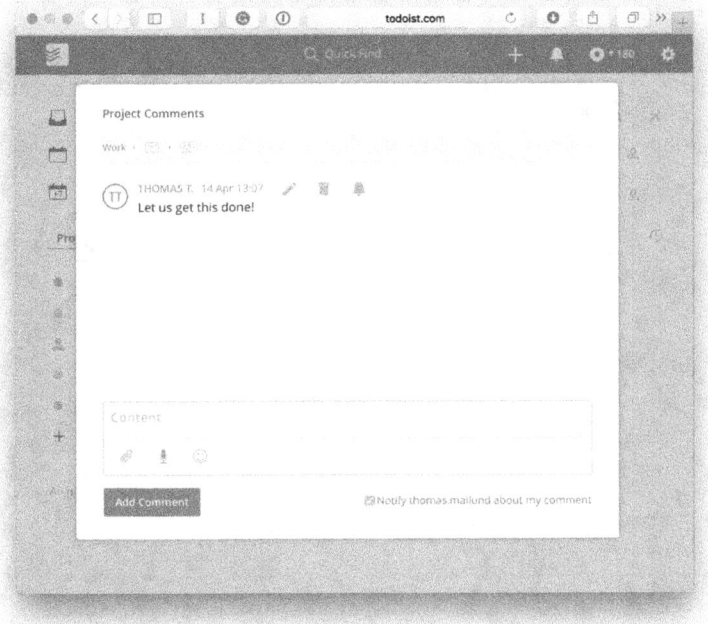

Figure 49: Project comment sent.

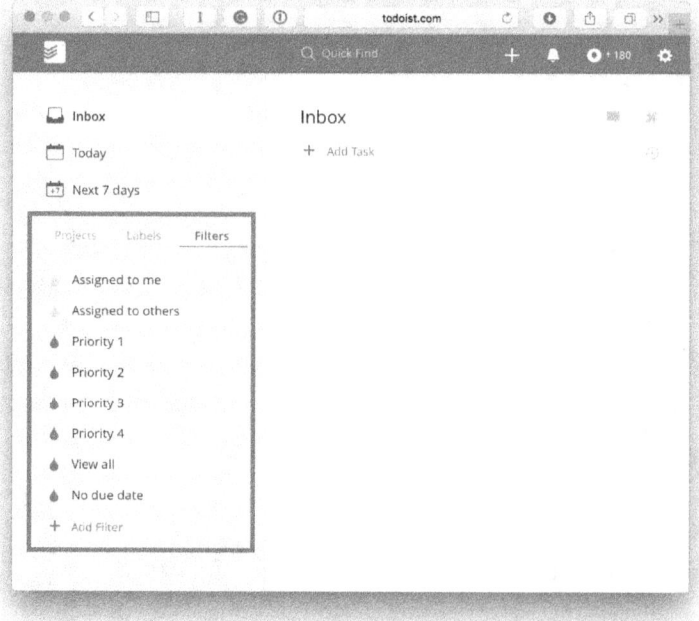

Figure 50: Filters.

Chapter **4**

Premium features

The basic features of a free Todoist account suffice for most users of Todoist, but with a premium subscription, you get extra features that enhance the user experience. We describe these features in this chapter. If you are not interested in having a premium subscription, you can skip to the next chapter.

Labels

Labels provide an alternative and orthogonal way of organising your tasks. While you already know how to use projects to group related tasks together, tasks often have different relationships depending on how you look at them. Some are related because of their due date or priority. Others are related because of the location you must be in to handle tasks—at home, at the office, out shopping. Some tasks can be grouped based on how much effort it will take to handle them—some

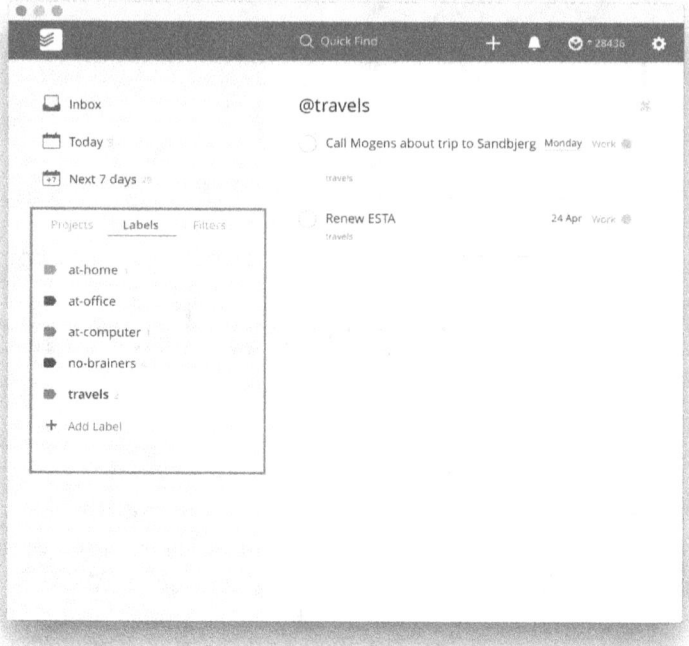

Figure 51: Labels.

might require several hours to get into the flow while others you can handle whenever you have a few minutes free. These kinds of similar tasks can be grouped together using labels.

You can get the list of labels you have associated with your tasks by clicking Labels to the right of Projects in the bottom-left pane of the Todoist window.

In the example shown here, labels are used to group tasks that must be performed at home, at the office, and/or when sitting at a computer. Another label is used for tasks that can be handled when there is a little bit of free time ("no brainers") that is useful for when there is a break between meetings but not time enough to get deep into a project. Theres also a label for organising travels, where some planning might be needed ahead of time.

You can explicitly define which labels you want to use—just click Add Label for each category you want—but you can also define a new label when you add a task to Todoist. When you write the title of a task you can type "@" to start adding a label. After that, just type the label you want to associate with the task. You will be able to autocomplete on existing labels, but you can add a new one this way as well.

After adding a label, the label will be highlighted in the task description.

You can add as many labels as you want.

Incidentally, projects can be assigned when creating a task in a similar way by using "#" instead of "@". Just press "#" and type a project name. Again, you can autocomplete on an existing project or type a new project name and create the project when you add the task.

If you move your pointer over a label name, you see three dots that you can use to bring up a menu for a label. All you can really do with labels is delete them or edit them.

The only thing you can "edit" about labels, though, is the colour associated with them.

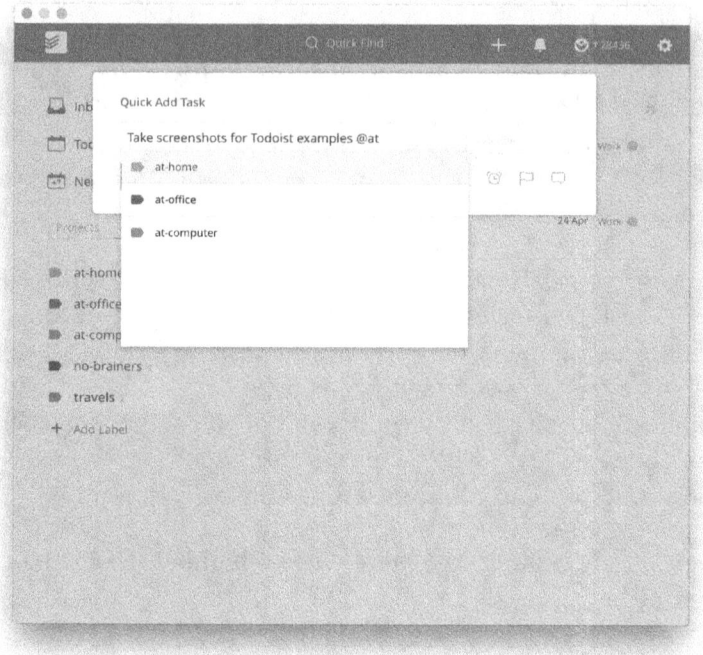

Figure 52: Quick-add a task with a label.

Filters

With a premium subscription, you can turn filters into a much more powerful tool by customising them. With a basic subscription, you are stuck with the ones that are already defined, but with a premium subscription you can add new filters and use them to show tasks matching a query. You can use the query language described in the Todoist manual and

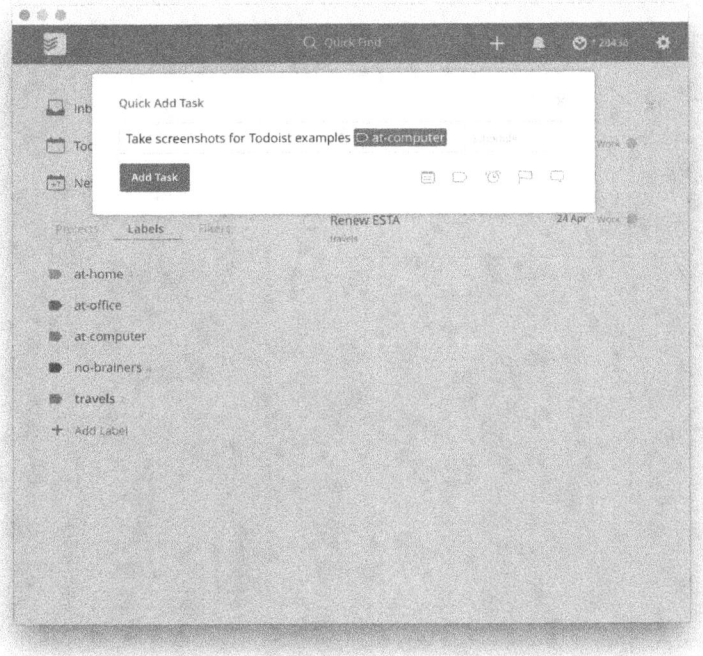

Figure 53: Highlighted label.

filter by labels, projects, priority and due dates. Below we show an example where we define a filter for upcoming travels. We specify a query that matches all tasks with the `@travels` label and that are due within the next 30 days. The tasks matching the query are shown in the list on the right.

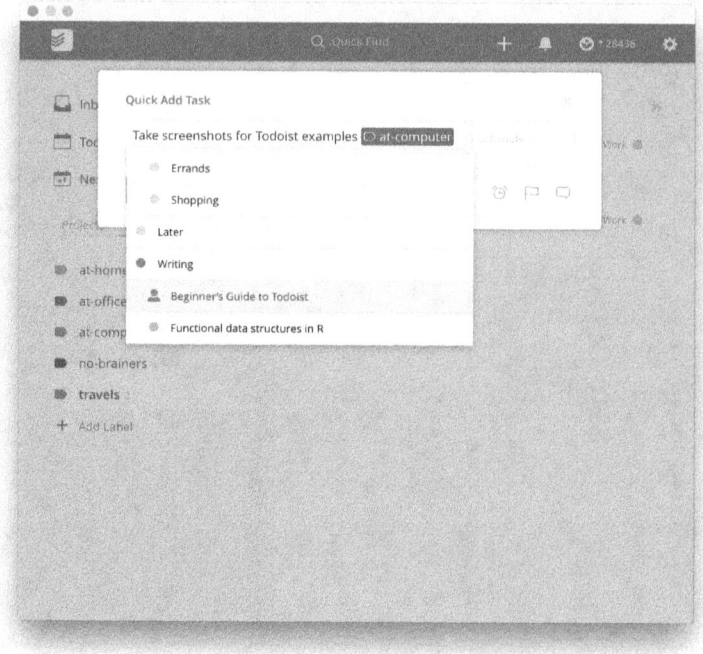

Figure 54: Adding a task with both a label and a project.

Reminders

With a premium subscription, you can also get reminders from Todoist. There are three different types of reminders: automatic reminders, explicit reminders, and location reminders.

Automatic reminders are used when you assign a time as well as a date to a task. If you do, you will receive a reminder about the task 30 minutes before the due date. You can change the

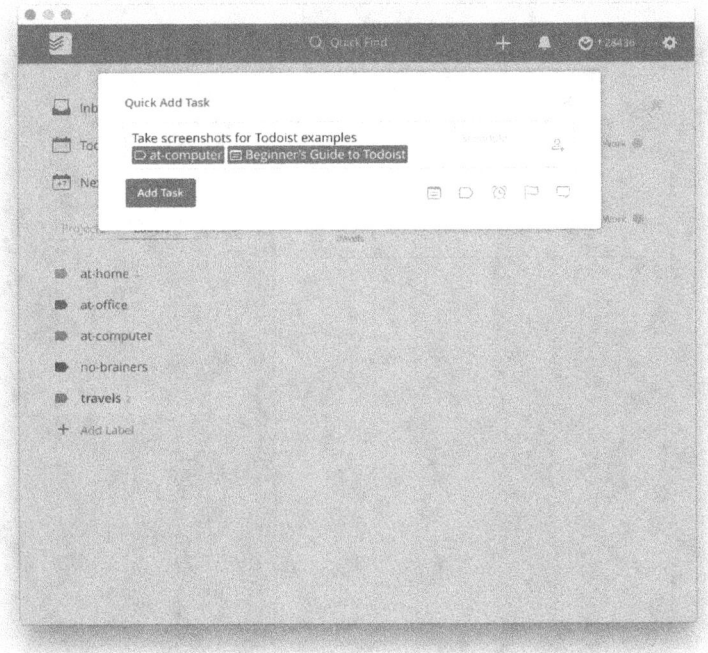

Figure 55: Both label and project highlighted.

default time by going to Settings and then Reminders.

How you receive reminders depends on the platform you are using. If you only use the web version of Todoist, you will need to set up text messages or emails to make sure you get a notification, but if you set up Todoist on a mobile device—iOS or Android—you can get notifications right on your device to ensure you never miss a reminder.

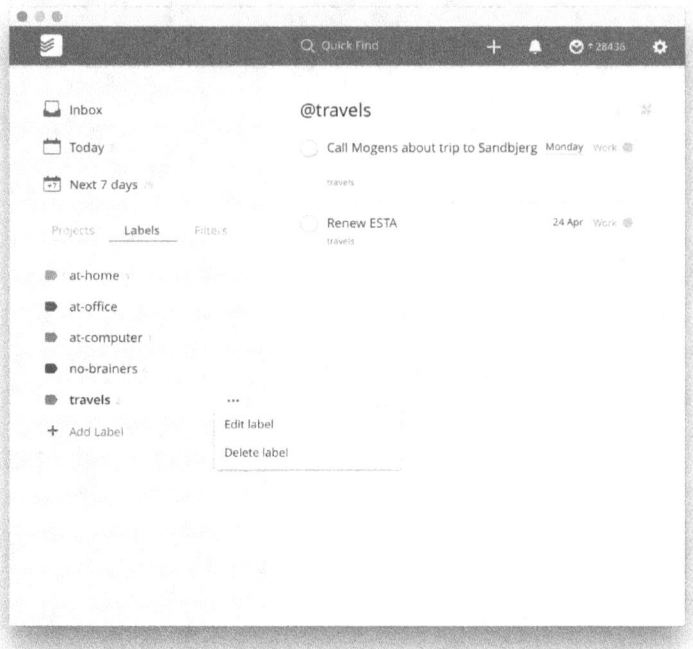

Figure 56: Selecting label options.

Automatic reminders will handle many common tasks, but receiving a reminder 30 minutes—or whatever you choose in your settings—might not be optimal for tasks that you might have to worry about days before their deadlines. When the automatic reminder does not suffice, you can set reminders explicitly.

When you are adding a task to Todoist, you can click on the alarm clock under the task title to set a custom reminder.

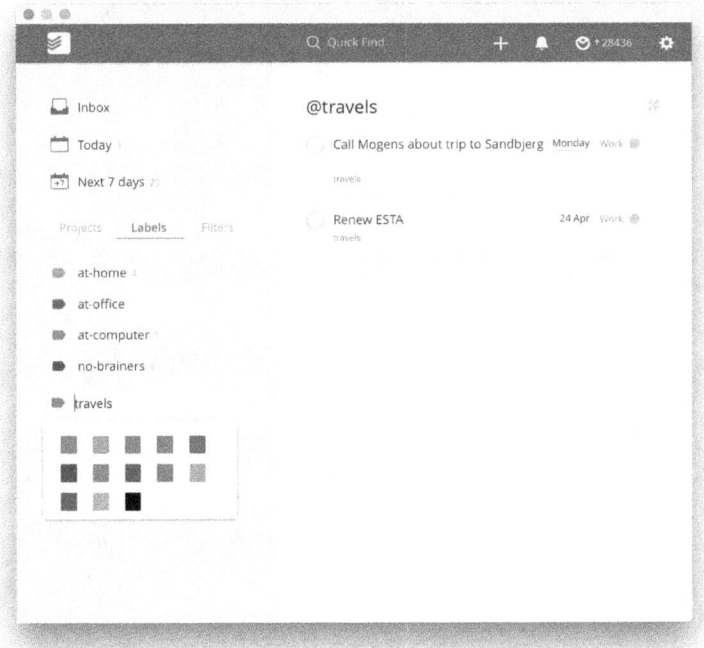

Figure 57: Editing a label.

This opens up a field where you can specify a reminder. By default, the reminder is a date and time reminder as shown by the clock icon to the left. You can specify whatever date and time you would like for a reminder. The other type of reminder is a location based reminder, which we will describe in detail below.

After setting a reminder, you will automatically open a field for adding another one. Press ESC to abort the next reminder

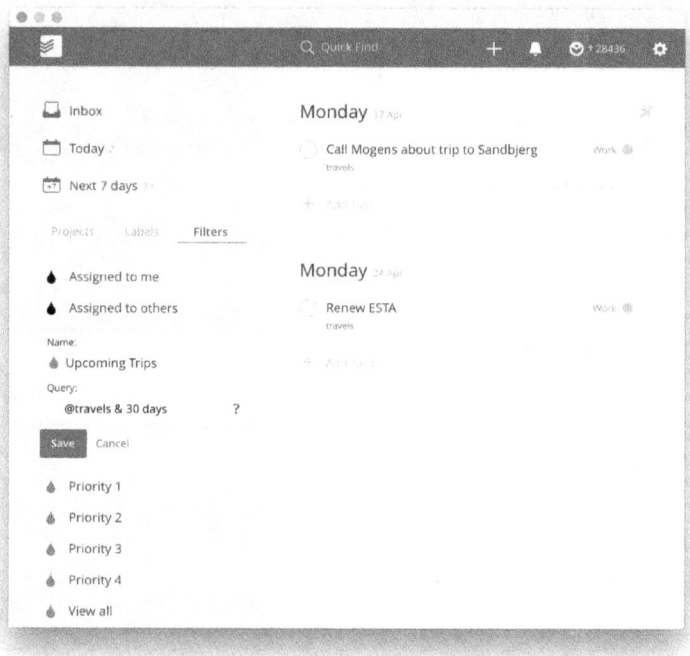

Figure 58: Custom filters.

to finish adding reminders, or type in as many as you want.

A task with reminders associated will be shown with an alarm clock icon to the right of its title.

If you have a mobile device with Todoist on it, you can also use location awareness to set up reminders when you enter or when you leave a location.

To set up a location reminder, you need to add a reminder

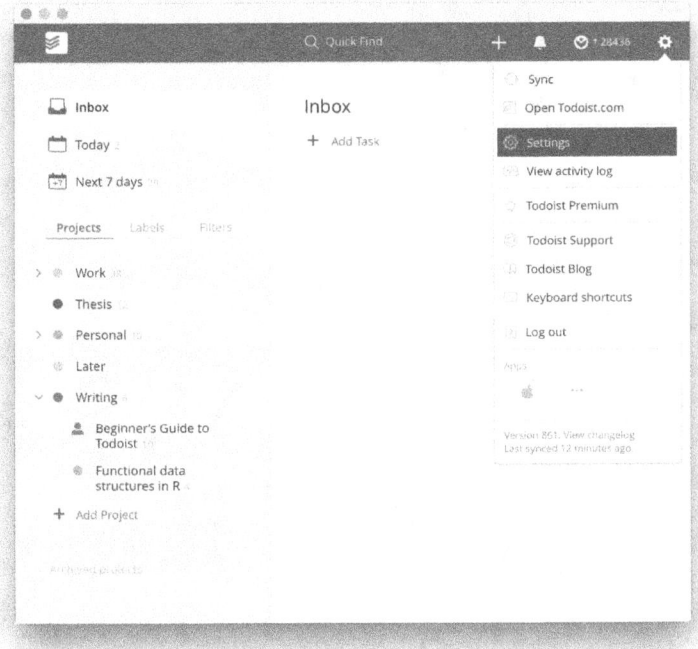

Figure 59: Opening settings.

as before, but you should click the clock icon to change the reminder from being associated with a given time to being associated with a location.

For the actual location, you need to type in an address. You can also specify whether you want the reminder when you arrive at the location, or when you leave.

Once you have added a reminder, you will automatically start

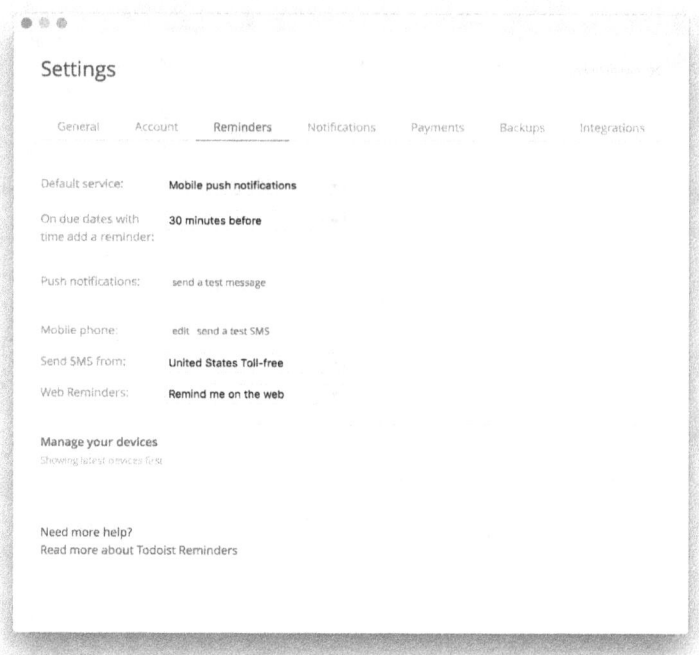

Figure 60: Reminder settings.

making another, and again you can press ESC to finish adding them.

If you want a location reminder with a location you have used before, you can click the icon to the right of the address field and select a recent location.

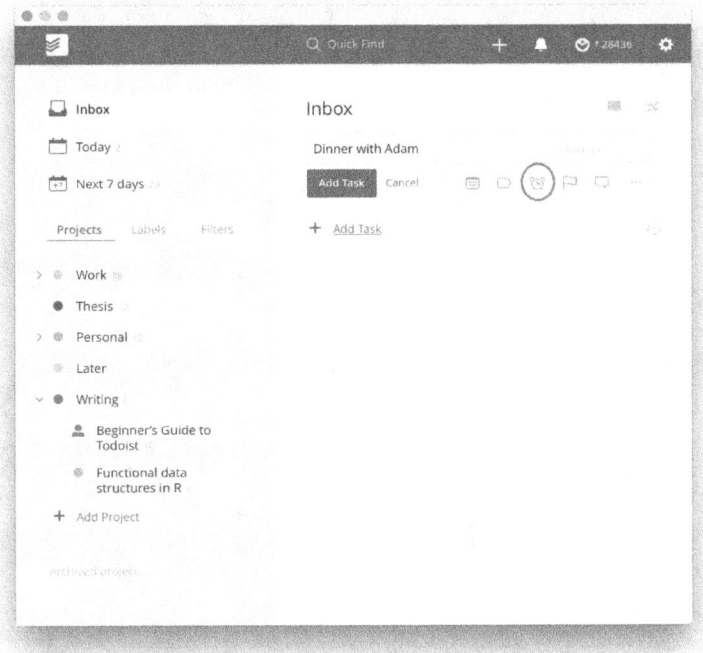

Figure 61: Setting a custom reminder.

Comments and file uploads

You can add additional information to both projects and tasks using comments. You can get access to project comments by clicking the dialogue icon next to a project title.

You can then write a text as a comment, upload a file, or add a recording.

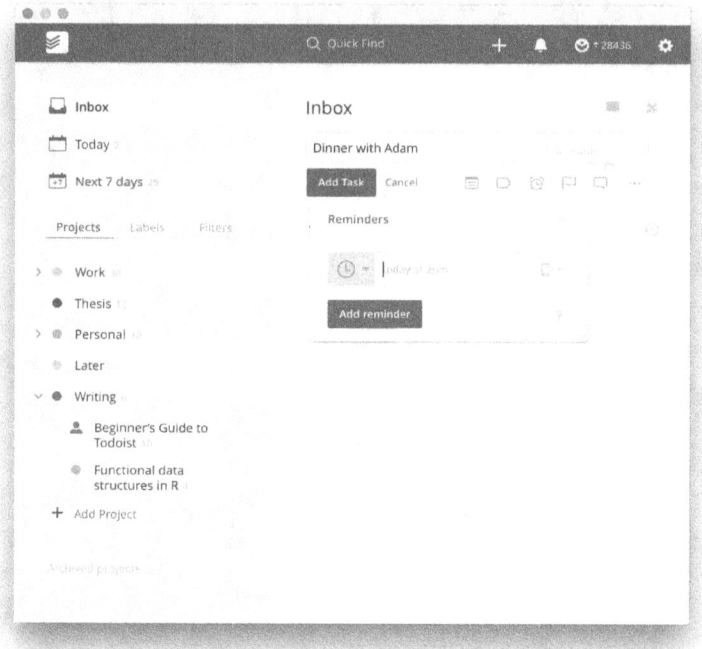

Figure 62: Input for custom reminders.

Files you upload will be shown together with text comments.

Project comments are also how you can communicate with your collaborators in a shared project.

You can add task comments by clicking on the dialogue icon next to a task title—if there are no comments associated with a task, you will need to move your pointer there before the icon appears.

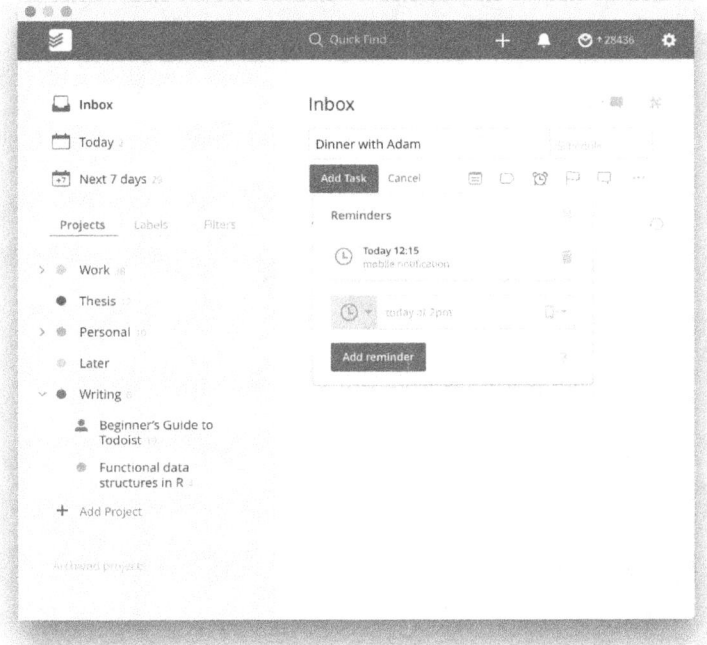

Figure 63: After adding one reminder.

Adding a comment to a task works just as adding a comment to a project.

The number of comments added to a project or a task will be shown next to their comment icons.

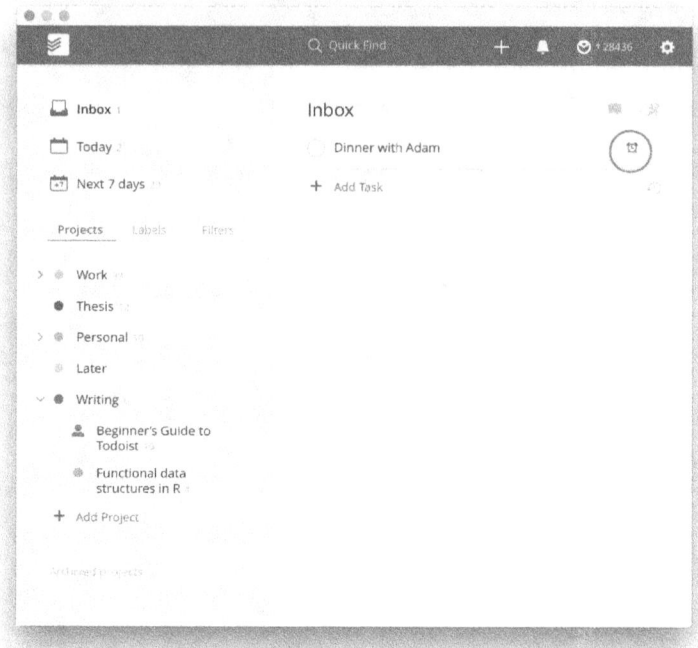

Figure 64: Alarm clock indicates a reminder time.

Integration with mail and calendars

Also available as premium features are integration with mail and calendars. You can access these features inside a project view by clicking on the tools icon to the right of the project title, or from the project list menu on the left.

The mail integration gives you an email address that you can use to add tasks to a project via emails. Sending emails to

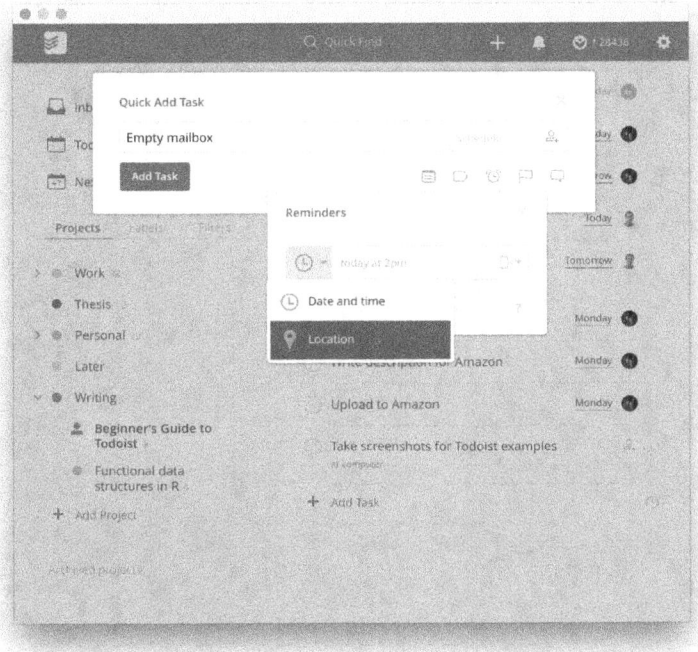

Figure 65: Selecting a location reminder.

this address will construct a task in the project. You can specify priorities, labels, and dates from the subject or body of the email.

Adding tasks via emails might not seem that useful compared to just adding tasks directly to Todoist, but it is a convenient way of making tasks out of emails: you can forward emails to relevant Todoist projects and add meta information in the forwarded email's body. Attachments and the forwarded

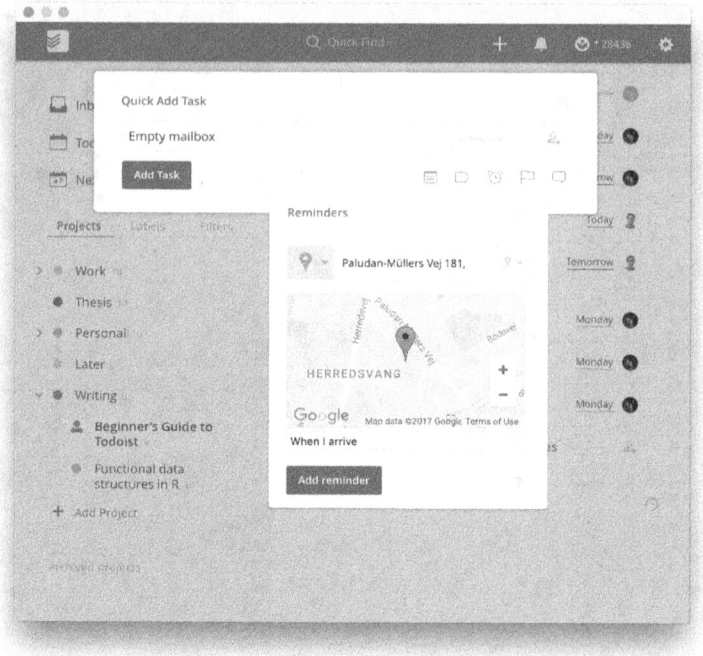

Figure 66: Location reminder at an address.

email will be added as comments to the task you create this way.

Calendar integration gives you a calendar feed you can subscribe to that will show you your tasks. You can select to show all tasks or just the tasks within one project. Once integrated, tasks in a project you subscribe to will be shown on their due dates in your calendar program.

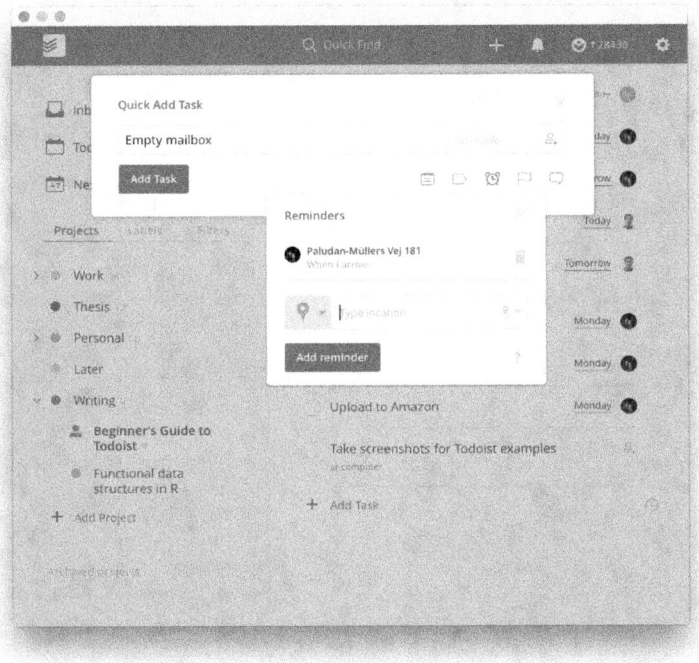

Figure 67: Ready for more reminders.

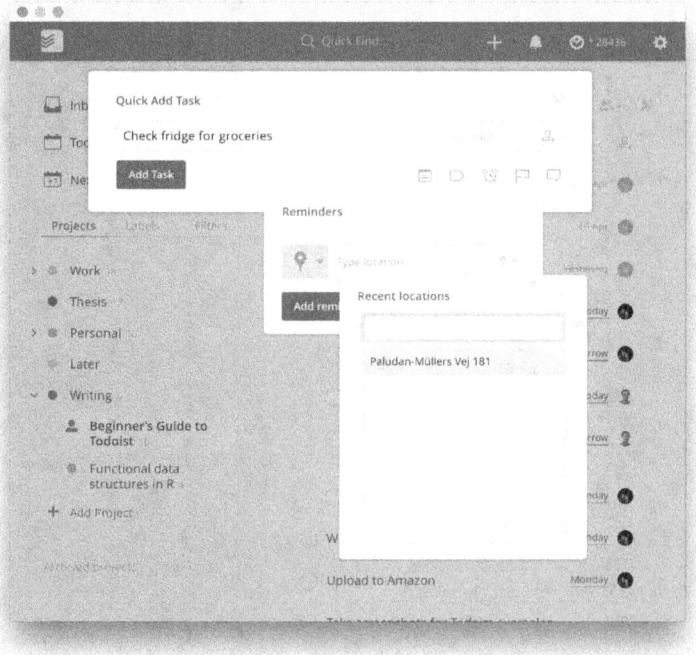

Figure 68: Recent locations.

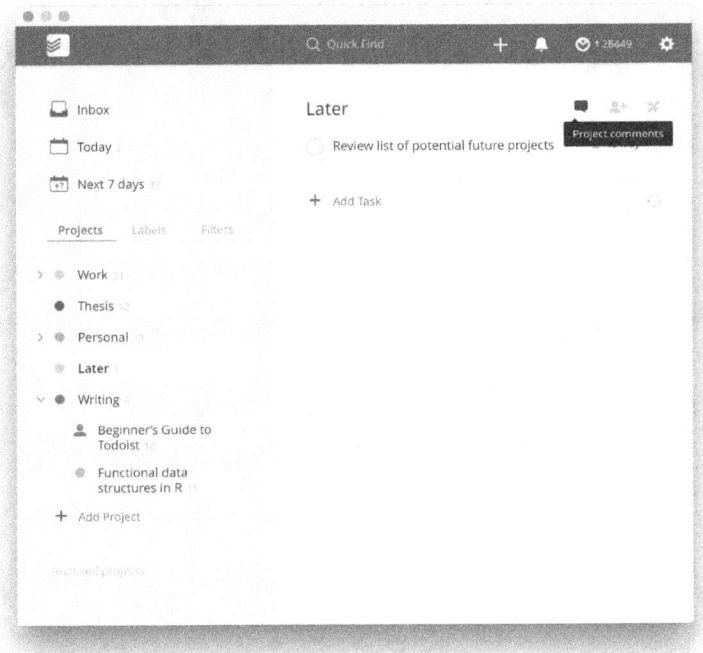

Figure 69: Adding a comment to a project.

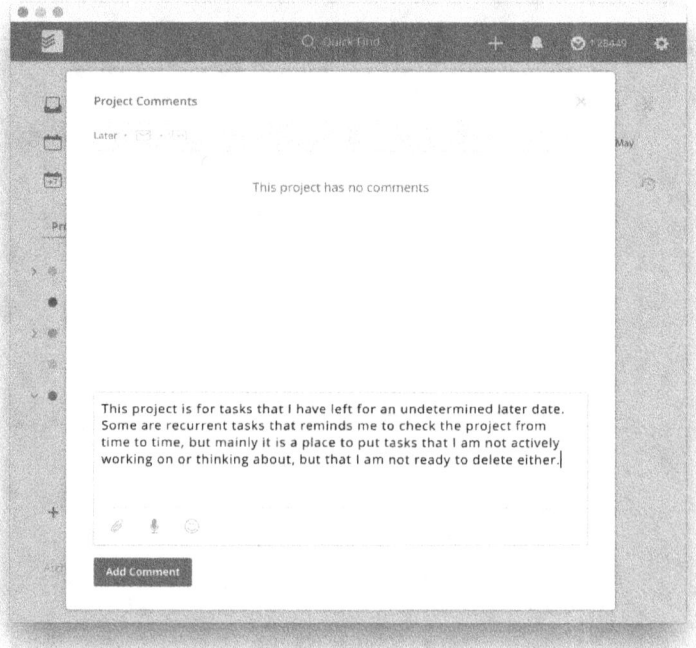

Figure 70: Writing a comment.

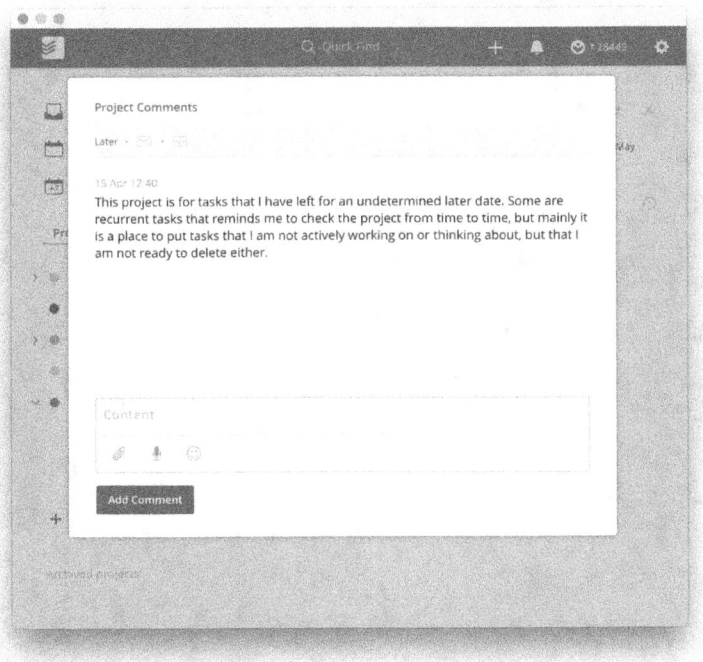

Figure 71: A comment once it is sent.

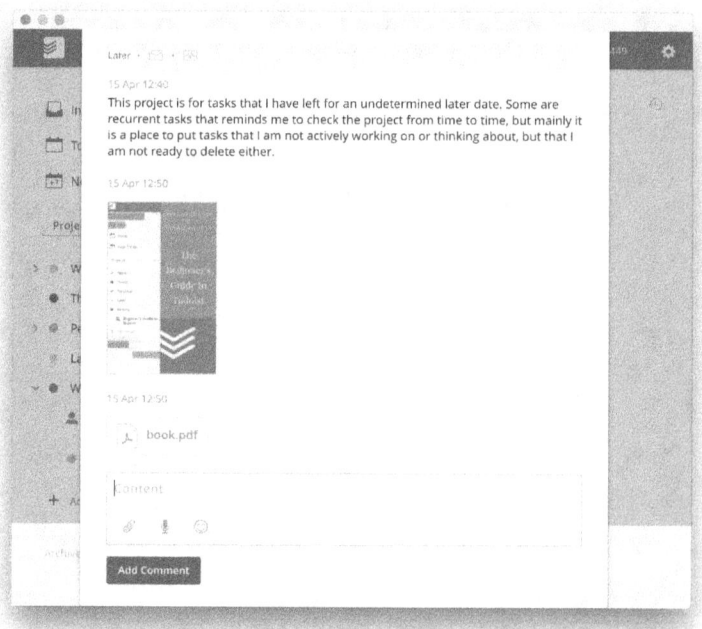

Figure 72: A comment with a picture attached.

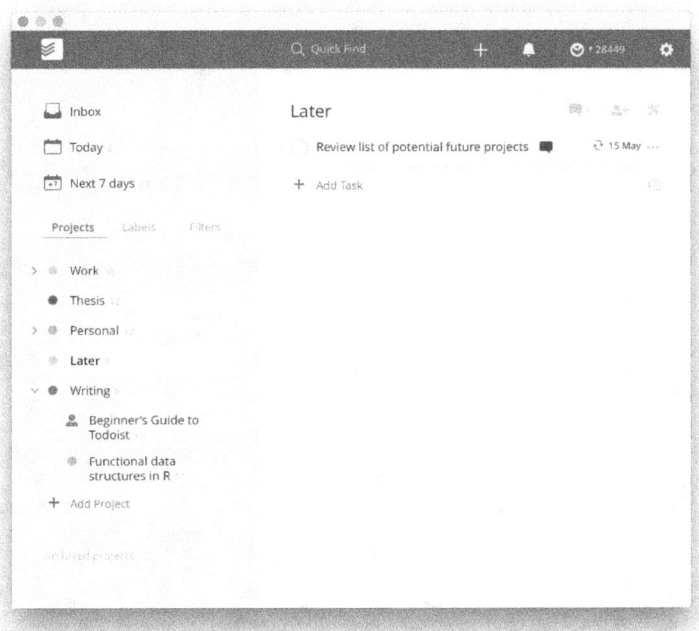

Figure 73: A task comment.

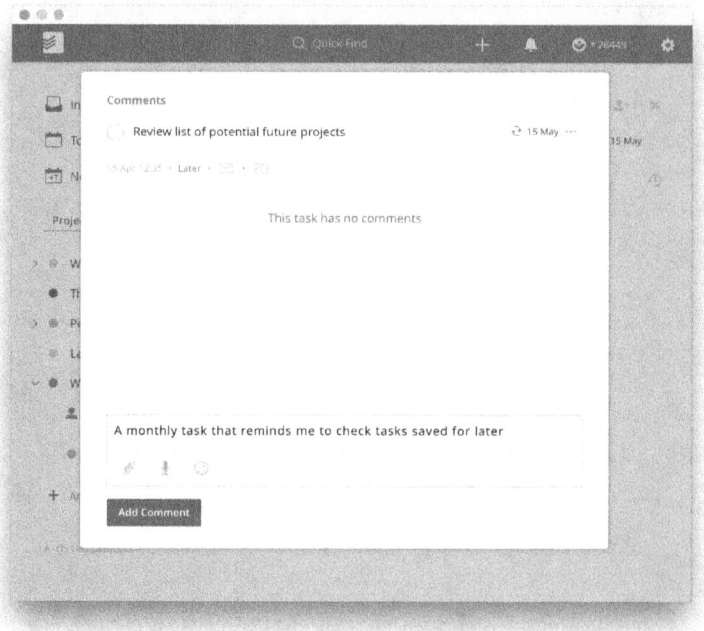

Figure 74: Writing a comment.

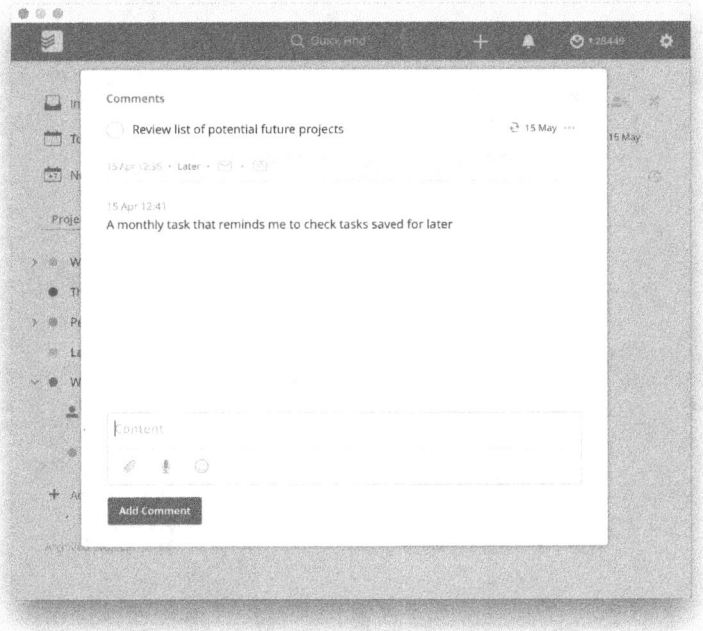

Figure 75: Submitted comment.

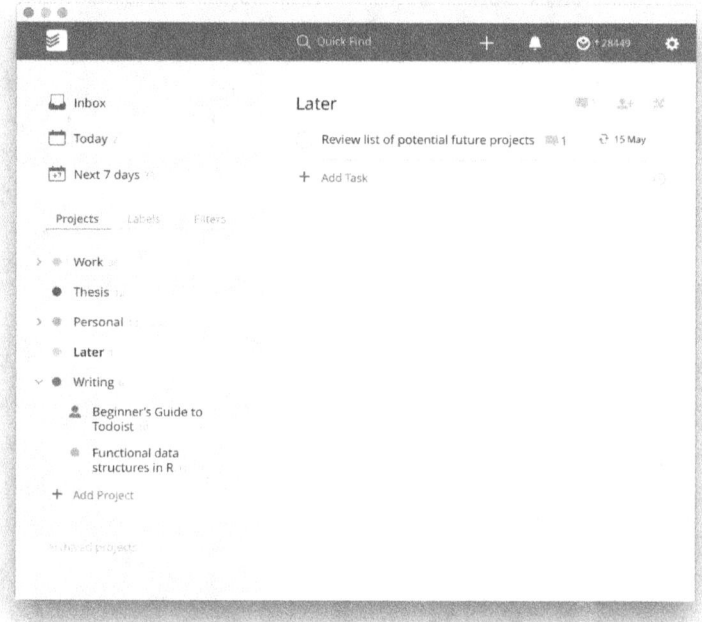

Figure 76: Comment counter.

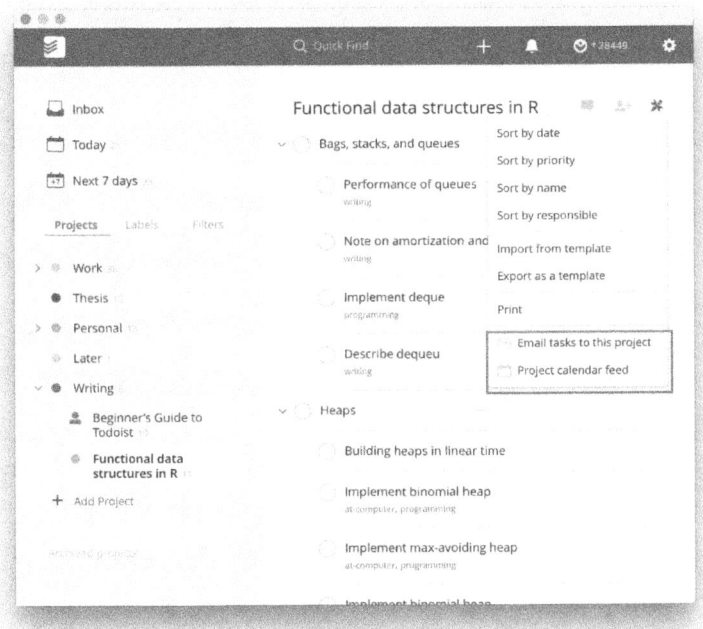

Figure 77: Email settings from inside a project.

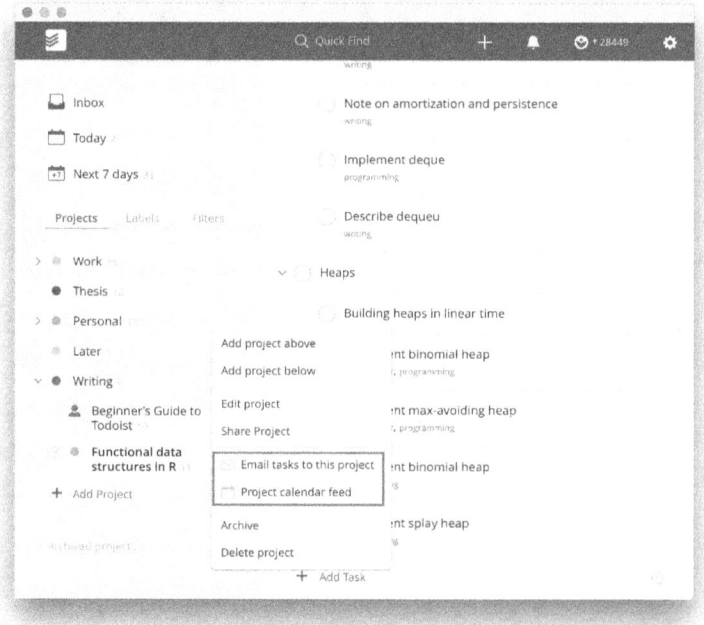

Figure 78: Email settings from the projects list.

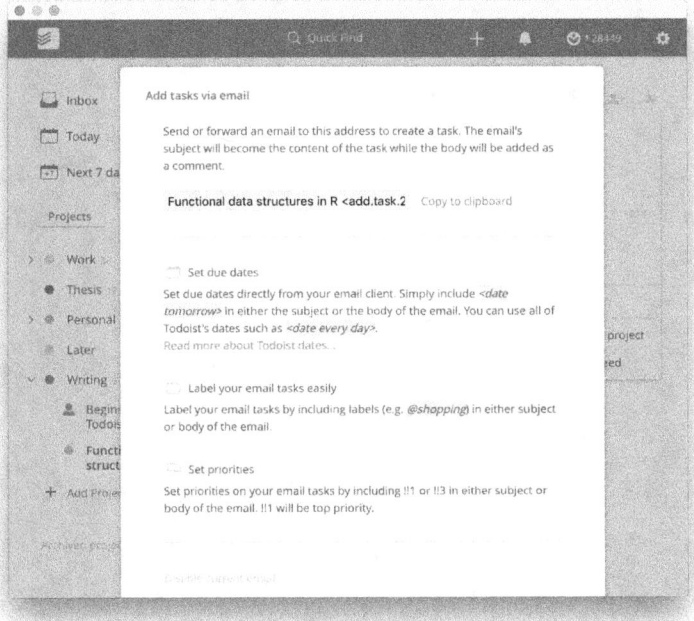

Figure 79: Email settings.

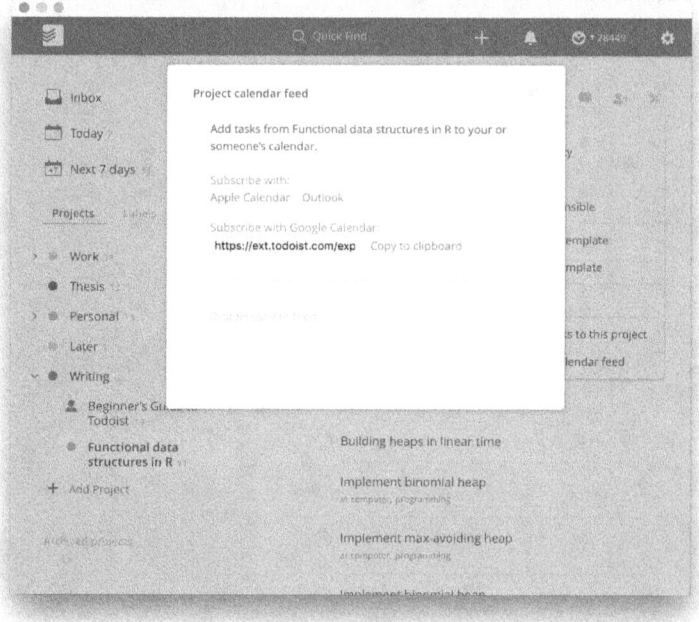

Figure 80: Calendar integration.

Chapter 5

Integrations

Todoist integrates with hundreds of different apps to enable you to get an overarching view of all your tasks across services – it's a great way to get complete control of your life. In this chapter, we'll briefly look at various integrations and how you can utilise them to become more organised and productive. You can find a full list on Todoist's integrations page.

Mail integrations

People spend 28% or more of their time at work sending and receiving email. Spending some energy on becoming better at emailing will save you a lot of time.

Use Todoist for Gmail or Todoist for Outlook to easily add emails as tasks and manage your to-do list directly from your email client. When you add emails as tasks, you keep your inbox clean and have the ability to add due dates, reminders, and priorities to your emails (and see them with all the other tasks you have). We recommend that you use the Inbox Zero workflow in combination with the Todoist plugin to keep your inbox as clear as possible and reduce the distractions of seeing hundreds of unread emails everytime you check your mail.

Browser extensions

Todoist's browser extensions let you add any website as a task and manage your todo-list without leaving the site you are visiting.

You can use this to keep track of articles you want to read, books that are interesting, an Amazon.com shopping list, or even a tweet you want to respond to later.

Install Todoist for Chrome or Todoist for Firefox and get started easily.

Speak to your personal assistant

Todoist integrates directly with Alexa or Google Assistant and lets you easily add tasks from anywhere in your home by just speaking. Many people find this integration to feel like pure science-fiction and are even more surprised when it works extremely well.

For example, you can just say "Alexa, add pick up the kids tomorrow at 2 pm to my todo-list", and Alexa will add a task with a due date and a reminder to your Todoist project.

Learn how to start using Todoist for Alexa or Todoist for Google Assistant.

Time tracking using Toggl

In many professions, people are required to track the time they spend on each task for each particular client. Luckily, Todoist integrates with Toggl, one of the most popular time tracking services. The Toggl integration enables you to easily keep track of how much time you are spending on your tasks.

Automate your life using IFTTT and Zapier

Todoist integrates with IFTTT and Zapier, some of the most popular automation tools. These tools enable you to create incredibly sophisticated and useful workflows between hundreds of different apps.

To give you an idea of how powerful this is let's look at an example. Let's say you are a surfer and you would like to get reminded a day before the waves are going to be good. How would you solve this? Well, an easy way is to connect Surfline and Todoist on IFTTT. You can create an applet that adds a task to your #Surf project a day before the surf will be good at your local surf spot! The likelihood of you being a surfer isn't high, but hopefully, you get the point of how powerful this is.

Zapier even supports multi-step workflows involving many apps giving you very powerful Todoist workflows.

It's only your imagination that sets a limit on what things you can automate and integrate with each other.

Chapter **6**

Working efficiently with your Inbox and your projects

The goal of using a todo list to keep track of your daily tasks is to increase your productivity, but there is an overhead involved: organising your tasks. If you leave all your tasks in one big pile, it becomes a mess that doesn't help you, but on the other hand, it also takes time to organise the tasks into projects. It's ideal to have a process to be as efficient as possible when it comes to organizing your tasks.

During a busy day, there are likely to be many tasks you think of or are asked to do and your instinct would be to put these tasks on your todo list before you forget about them. However, you may not have the time and shouldn't necessarily organise the tasks at the same time as you add them to your list. It takes some effort to figure out whether these tasks are part of a project, which priority the tasks have and when you need to have them done. You can't necessarily make those decisions if you're in the middle of some important work, and too much thinking would break the flow of what you are doing. You don't want to let the todo list become a burden rather than a boon.

What you want to do is to add tasks as soon as you think of them, but make it a daily task to organise them when you have time. Perhaps you could set aside half an hour at the end of the day, or ten minutes in the morning over your coffee, to go through new tasks and organise them. In Todoist, the Inbox is there to assist you with this. Whenever you think of a new task, add it to the Inbox project and don't worry about organizing the task any further. Instead, set some time aside each day to go through the Inbox and organise the new tasks there.

Some tasks are easier to organize than others. Some tasks obviously belong in certain projects, like a grocery list. Some, obviously, have higher priorities than others. Some have deadlines that you have to meet. Overall, organising different tasks and adding tasks to your todo list requires varying levels of mental effort. That's why you need a great Inbox process.

Using your Inbox

Every time you think of a task, add it to your Inbox project. Small or large, important or not, large task or small, it doesn't matter. Just keep adding everything you can think of when you think of it, day in, day out. What you want to do is to offload the effort your brain uses in remembering future tasks to your todo list. If you are anything like us, you probably have tasks running around your brain constantly reminding you about their existence, regardless of how important they are. You may be in a constant state of not wanting to forget anything that might be important. This is where a todo list can be a life saver. As soon as you think of a task, add it to your todo list, and stop spending brain power thinking about it.

Of course, writing down tasks doesn't mean that you have achieved them, so there is an important second step if you want to stop worrying about forgetting important tasks. You have to keep them organised and make sure that you accomplish them. Organising the tasks is the important second step—actually doing the tasks is a third, and much more important, step, but that will follow from organising the tasks properly.

So now that you have all your tasks in your Inbox, when you go through the tasks at the end of the day or the next morning, you have separated recording your tasks from the act of organising them. You'll find that the organisation becomes less of a burden, and it might even become enjoyable. This is a lot better than constantly breaking your workflow.

In short, record everything and don't worry about—at this time—how important or how trivial a task is. Just record it. Then, once a day, go through your Inbox and evaluate each task.

So how do you organize tasks?

Just go through each task. The first question you want to ask yourself is whether the task is worth doing or not. During a busy day, every task seems important, but in actuality, not all tasks are. Some, when you think about them away from the heat of the moment, can just be deleted. The are not important after all. Some, on the other hand, you still want to do, but they are not important to do right now—you don't want to forget about them, but there is not need to worry about them just yet. Put those in a "later" project and look at that folder once in a while to see which tasks are still worth keeping, which tasks are actually important and need to be moved to a more prominent place, and what tasks should be deleted because they just aren't important any longer.

When you go through your Inbox, you will find many tasks that belong to obvious projects. Those, you can move there. But don't just move them there; take some time to think about how important they are for that project. Give the tasks a priority. Don't worry too much about the priority you give to tasks—you can always change them, after all—but a rough idea about how important a task is will help you organise a project down the line.

Some tasks do not necessarily belong to an obvious project. Those tasks are harder to organise. Fortunately, you have time to think about this since you are looking at them at during your "organising time". You don't have to make quick decisions. Figure out to which project they matter most, or consider whether they indicate that you need to create a new project to assign them to. You don't want too many projects—that makes organising your tasks harder—but if you find that there are tasks that keep popping up, that seem related, it is a good indication that you might want to create a new project to organise them into.

As you go through the tasks, you might want to give them all a deadline, so you don't forget about them. That is not necessarily a good idea. If we record that a task should be done by tomorrow, we give it more importance tomorrow than it necessarily has. We just tend to give deadlines more importance than the actual impact of tasks for a project. Many deadlines we give for tasks at the spur of the moment are completely arbitrary anyway—don't give tasks deadlines unless they are hard deadlines force upon you from external forces. Priorities are a better way to measure how important tasks are, but if you give even low priority tasks a deadline, you will tend to value the deadlines over the priorities.

Now, you might fear that if you don't give a task a deadline, which means they won't pop up on your Today list at any time, you will forget about them. That might be true, but if you never get to a task because there are always more important tasks—tasks with a higher priority—then you will often be making the right choice to work on the highest priority item. However, you should revisit your lists every once in a while to make sure to see whether any tasks in waiting now need a deadline or a priority boost. Just make sure you give them deadlines because the deadlines matter; not because you feel like completing them or so you don't forget about them.

Unless a task has a hard deadline, don't assign one to it. Give it a priority and assign it to a project. You will go back to each project regularly anyway and evaluate the tasks there.

Working with your projects

How you work with projects will be somewhat subjective. You have to evaluate regularly how important each project is to you. That is, of course, influenced by both external and internal factors, by work and family and by your personal goals. Regardless how important individual projects are, they are the highest level at which you want to organise your todo list. A high priority task in one project might be less important than a low priority task in a more important project. And how high a priority you give to a given project will vary from day to day—personal projects matter more in your time off than work projects while work projects are what you want to focus on during work hours.

A productive way to work with your todo list is to set aside time to work on individual projects rather than individual tasks. Deadlines might determine which projects you should be working on at any particular day—which is why we recommend that you don't put deadlines on tasks that are not hard deadlines—but more often, the importance of the actual project is what drives your work any individual day. If you set aside a fixed amount of time to work on each project during a day or a week then you simply will do the most important work for a given project at the time you set aside to work on that project. Use your calendar to set aside time to work on your important projects—that isn't something you want to use a todo list to do—and at the time you have set aside for a project, check out the most important tasks in that project. That is where your priorities will save you a lot of time – you can dive right into the task instead of thinking about what to work on first.

Of course, priorities change over time, so don't get too settled with the priority you give a task when you move it from your Inbox to a project. Priorities are always relative to all other tasks in a project, and once in a while, you want to go through your projects to reevaluate the priorities you have assigned to your tasks. If you want to work efficiently on a project, you can't just attack one task at a time—you also need to take the time to evaluate how important other tasks are and whether you want to attack them in groups. And you have to update those priorities regularly.

Taking time from accomplishing tasks to organise tasks might feel counterproductive, but you don't want to spend time on working on irrelevant tasks when more important tasks are ignored. That might feel productive, but in the long run, it isn't. To be productive, you have to set time aside to evaluate the importance of your tasks from time to time. How often you want to do this depends on your projects. Projects you work on every day, you probably want to look over once a week; other projects, once a month; other projects still, once a year. It all depends on how often you decide on which next task to work on. You want to look over your projects regularly enough that you are reasonably certain that any given task you work on is still important for the project.

Breaking down tasks

To work efficiently with your todo list, you need to break down your tasks into manageable bites. Tasks such as "design a homepage", "write a report" or "implement an algorithm" might be clear enough, but they are rarely easy to get started on. When you go through your projects to evaluate the tasks in them, ask yourself this question for each of them: Is this a task I know how to get started on? If you don't see what the next step is for a given task, it probably is too abstractly defined—you want to break it down into more manageable pieces. At the very least, you want to figure out what the first step of such a task would be.

Part of keeping a project organised is breaking down tasks into manageable bits that you can attack. Ideally, you want a session working on a project to consist of picking off the next task, completing it, and then moving to the next. You cannot do this if you first have to figure out what each task consist of; which subtasks you have to complete to deal with the task.

It is not that important if you spend time breaking down tasks into manageable sub-tasks during the time you have set aside to work on a project or during the time you have set aside for organising your project. What is important is that you actually do it so you can work efficiently with your todo list. If the tasks you put in your list are abstract and difficult to start, you will feel lost when you move from one task to another. Whenever you have an unmanageable task, take some time to figure out how it can be split into subtasks that are more easily done.

Chapter **7**

Systemist: A workflow example

One of the hardest things about adopting a productivity tool isn't learning to use the tool itself, but having a reliable productivity workflow. In this chapter, we want to introduce you to Systemist, a workflow developed by Amir over the past ten years.

Why would you have a workflow?

A productivity workflow is a collection of patterns you use to organise yourself. In the beginning, adopting a workflow might feel strange, but after a while, it will be running on auto-pilot, and you will be able to focus on completing important tasks instead of managing them (or forgetting about them).

The truth is that our lives and the world we live in are too complicated to just wing things. A reliable system can help you prioritise the important things and juggle many things at once without feeling overwhelmed and stressed.

Systemist

Systemist is a simplified workflow built for the modern world. Systemist works best with Todoist, given that the workflow was actually built around the app itself, but it can work with most other productivity apps as well. The core principles are much more important than the tools.

Systemist has six simple components.

1) Take it everywhere

A productivity system is only useful if you can access it everywhere you are. Luckily, Todoist has invested a lot of resources into making the service available everywhere. It's recommended installing Todoist on every device you have (mobile devices, web browsers, email clients, desktops): Todoist Apps

2) Capture everything

A productivity system is only useful if it captures all the important things going on in both your personal and professional life. Capturing everything gives you a lot of freedom to not stress that you will forget something important (for example, a follow-up with a client, buying a gift, etc.) It will also give you a complete overview of things you need to do.

Here are some of the things you can capture:

- Follow-ups you need to do, whether its with your teammates or with people external to your organization.
- Complex projects that have many smaller steps.
- A shared shopping list with your partner.
- Emails you can't answer them right away. You can use Todoist for Gmail or Outlook.
- A shared release list with your colleagues.
- Recurring tasks to check up on long-term projects you are doing.
- Web pages you can't get to right away. Could be adding an Amazon item you want to buy, adding an IMDB movie to your movie list, or saving articles to read later (Todoist for Chrome).
- A "Hiring" project of people you want to hire.
- Bug reports that are related to you.
- Health-related tasks (for example, weekly gym and running sessions).
- Etc.

Everything you need to do should be inside your system!

3) Break it up into small tasks and make them actionable

Small tasks are easier to complete than big ones, so break big tasks into some smaller sub-tasks that can be completed in 1 hour or less. This will allow you to estimate the total time involved more accurately. Plus, you'll see progress as you check things off.

It's also critical to make things actionable. You should be able to complete everything you have on your todo list. Don't keep items that you can't or don't plan to complete.

4) Prioritize

Todoist offers great tools to help you prioritise your days. Here's how you can use these with Systemist:

- Use due dates to specify when you want to complete something. Schedule a low priority task for the future. A high priority task could be scheduled for today or tomorrow.
- Use Todoist's priority levels to prioritise daily tasks. This is super useful in the daily/weekly views as Todoist will automatically put higher priority tasks first.
- Use labels to add even more prioritisation. For example, you could use a [@high_impact] label on tasks that will create a high impact. The great thing about label is that you can easily filter them across all of your projects

5) Get to to-do list zero daily

With Systemist you would want to use "To-do list Zero". The idea was inspired by Inbox Zero, and it's quite simple: At the end of the day, you want zero tasks on your today list.

The truth is that most days you won't complete everything on your today list and you will most likely postpone things. Not completing everything isn't a negative thing; it's an opportunity to take stock of your tasks, re-evaluate them, and then re-plan them.

"To-do list Zero" keeps the system tidy, up-to-date, and, most importantly, manageable.

6) Get consistent feedback

Most productivity systems only focus on what you need to do and not what you have done. Where's the fun if you don't celebrate progress and don't get insights into how productive you are?

That's why Todoist has Todoist Karma, a feedback system that gives you insights into your productivity and awards you for your accomplishments.

Todoist Karma tracks your progress, visualises it and gives you points. As a beginner, this system is quite fun, since there are also levels involved and you feel like you are progressing. Todoist Karma is like a mini-game that makes task management a bit more fun and rewarding.

After you reach a certain level, Karma becomes a bit boring. This is where goals and streaks kick in. You can set goals for the number of tasks you want to complete each day or week. For every goal you complete, Karma will increase your streak. If you miss a goal one day, your streak gets reset to zero. This system is inspired by Jerry Seinfeld's Productivity Secret.

Managing emails

We recommend following Inbox Zero. For example:

- Only check emails twice per day. Once in the morning and once in the afternoon.
- In each session, try to process all the emails.
- If you can, respond to an email right away. If you can't, turn it into a task with a due date and priority via Todoist for Gmail.

- Disable all notifications from your email client on all of you devices, so you won't be disturbed as you focus on other things.

Managing chat

Slack and other chat apps can be a huge productivity killer since they can interrupt you at any time. Studies have shown that the average desk job employee loses 2.1 hours a day to distractions and interruptions. That adds up to over a full day of work every week!

Here's how you deal with these messaging services:

- Only be online when you want to be interrupted. Shut down these apps when you need to do focused work.
- Try to process chat in batches. For example, check chat apps a few times per day (maybe once an hour or so).
- Disable all notifications from chat apps on mobile. (if people need to reach you then give them a phone number).

This workflow lets you get some work done without being interrupted all the time.

Other workflows

Todoist is quite versatile, and it works with most other workflows. Here's some of them:

- Getting Things Done [GTD]. There's a guide you can follow here on how to get GTD inside Todoist.

- Pomodoro with Todoist.

Chapter **8**

Afterword

We have now taken you through the basic features of Todoist and described how you might use this tool to increase your productivity. Of course, no software tool is a panacea and using Todoist will not automatically make you more productive, reduce your stress levels, or help you manage your many tasks. It only helps if you can integrate Todoist into your life and use it in ways that work naturally for you.

Using a todo-list has great potential, but you won't simply stop stressing because you write your tasks down—your brain knows those tasks are still out there. A todo-list process only starts working once your brain trusts you actually to return to finish the tasks on the todo-list. At first, don't worry if you're still thinking about tasks – your brain is not easy to fool and it will be skeptical.

We all know how it is when the brain is overloaded with everything it thinks it has to remember—you lie sleepless at night while your head swims with all tomorrow's tasks, next week's tasks, next month's tasks and all the stuff you have to remember to pack for your next trip. If you are in this situation, you will not believe us when we tell you that simply writing down tomorrow's tasks will take half of this stress away. You know and we know it doesn't happen like that.

You will have to start trusting that the tasks you write down are not worth worrying about until you check the list again later. Otherwise, your brain will still obsess about it while you try to sleep. Eventually, you will need to persuade your brain that the the todo-list is helpful and is acting as a secondary memory, and that it is time to get some sleep. Be patient, it takes time before you get comfortable with todo-lists and a bit longer before your brain will trust in them; your subconscience, running on the reptile brain, needs a lot more evidence before it trusts you.

Todo-lists, and Todoist, will help you manage a busy and demanding life, but only if you use it consistently. If you get into the habit of putting all the tasks you think of during the day into your todo-list, your brain will eventually accept this. It will be comfortable knowing that it doesn't have to keep remembering all the things you have to do—it knows that you have a list for remembering it—and you can start using that brain power for productive things rather than remembering every little task.

No software solution will help you get more productive as if by magic. You need to integrate it into your daily life, and that takes time. We evolved with one todo-list, one piece of software only, our human brain. It takes time to convince our reptile brain to accept a new reality. But it is possible to move beyond this. It just takes time and practice.

Try out Todoist for a little bit, but don't do it half-measured. If you only use it for a few important tasks, you might find a little relief, but you will not calm down your brain's version of its own todo-list. If you want to experience the full productivity gain of using todo-lists—and the calm it brings to you when you are not working on projects—you have to jump into it with both legs.

Give it a shot. Try to offload all the tasks you have to do, just for one month, to Todoist. Train your brain to accept that it is no longer your primary todo-list. If you manage for one month, you are never going back.

www.ingramcontent.com/pod-product-compliance
Lightning Source LLC
Chambersburg PA
CBHW071207220526
45468CB00002B/537